INDONESIAN
Dictionary & Phrasebook

Hippocrene Books
Dictionary & Phrasebooks

Albanian
Arabic (Eastern) *Romanized*
Arabic
Armenian, Eastern
Armenian, Western
Australian
Azerbaijani
Basque
Bosnian
Breton
British
Cajun French
Chechen
Chilenismos
Chinese
Croatian
Czech
Dari
Esperanto
Estonian
Finnish
French
Georgian
German
Greek
Gujarati
Hawaiian
Hebrew
Hindi
Hungarian
Igbo
Ilocaro
Irish
Italian
Japanese *Romanized*

Korean
Lao *Romanized*
Latvian
Lingala
Lithuanian
Malagasy
Maltese
Maya, Yucatec
Mongolian
Norwegian
Pashto
Pilipino (Tagalog)
Polish
Portuguese, Brazilian
Québécois
Romanian
Romansh
Russian
Serbian
Sicilian
Slovak
Slovene
Somali
Swedish
Tajik
Tamil
Turkish
Turkmen
Ukrainian
Urdu
Uzbek
Vietnamese
Welsh
Wolof

INDONESIAN
Dictionary & Phrasebook

INDONESIAN-ENGLISH

ENGLISH-INDONESIAN

Srinawati Salim

HIPPOCRENE BOOKS, INC.
New York, NY

For information, please contact:
    Hippocrene Books, Inc.
    171 Madison Avenue
    New York, NY 10016
    www.hippocrenebooks.com

Library of Congress Cataloging-in-Publication Data

    Salim, Srinawati.
        Indonesian dictionary & phrasebook : Indonesian-English,
    English-Indonesian / Srinawati Salim.
            p.   cm.
    ISBN-13: 978-0-7818-1137-8
    ISBN-10: 0-7818-1137-6
        1. Indonesian language—Conversation and phrase books—
    English. 2. Indonesian language—Dictionaries—English.
    3. English language—Dictionaries—Indonesian. I. Title.
    II. Title: Indonesian dictionary and phrasebook.

    PL5075.S185 2007
    423'.99221—dc22   2007018678

Printed in the United States of America.

CONTENTS

PREFACE

Indonesian, or *Bahasa Indonesia*, is the official language of the Republic of Indonesia. It is used by the schools, the mass media, and all other government services. However, even though Indonesian is the official language, it is spoken as a second language by the majority of Indonesia's population, who speak their regional dialects as a first language.

Indonesian is a phonetic language. The words are pronounced the way they are spelled. As such, foreign speakers generally find it easy to use.

This book is written primarily as a handy tool for travelers to Indonesia who wish to communicate with the inhabitants. The phrases are arranged according to specific situations, and each dictionary contains 1,500 entries providing extra vocabulary. For those who wish to know more about the basics of the Indonesian language, a brief grammar is also included.

For now, *Selamat Jalan* and *Selamat Belajar!*

Happy Voyage and Happy Learning!

Pronunciation Guide

Letter	Pronunciation
a	like the a (ah) in father
b	like the b in boat
b (*at the end of a word*)	like the p in trap
c	like the ch in chair
d	like the d in dear
d (*at the end of a word*)	like the t in cat
e	like the e in egg
g	like the g in go
h	like the h in heart
i	like the ee in seed
j	like the j in just
k	like the k in key
l	like the l in lamp
m	like the m in mother
n	like the n in near
ny	like the ny in canyon
o	like the o in orange
p	like the p in people
r	like the r in run
s	like the s in sun
t	like the t in table
u	like the u in rule
v	like the v in vase
w	like the w in water
y	like the y in you
z	like the z in zoo

There are a few rules to keep in mind when properly pronouncing Indonesian words. The first, as indicated above, is that the sounds of *b* and *d* are hardened into, respectively, those of *p* and *t* when they appear at the end of a word. One should also remember that the letters *k*, *p*, and *t* are not aspirated when pronounced in Indonesian.

In other words, one does not release a puff of air when pronouncing them like one does in English.

If a syllable ends with the letter *k*, the *k* is pronounced as a glottal stop, a sound produced in the back of the throat. It is similar to the syllable break in the English expression "uh-oh."

Stress is almost always on the next-to-last syllable of a base word. The one exception is when that syllable contains a *schwa* sound (pronounced "uh"). Then the stress is on the final syllable.

There are four Indonesian diphthongs or combined vowels. They are:

ai	like the ai in Thai
au	like the ow in how
oi	like the oi in coin
ua	like the wah in Swahili

A Brief Indonesian Grammar

Articles

There is no Indonesian equivalent of the English articles *a*, *an*, and *the*. The noun appears by itself regardless of its grammatically definite or indefinite status. For example, the word *buku* ("book") may mean "book," "a book," or "the book," depending on the context of the sentence:

Whose <u>book</u> is this?
<u>Buku</u> siapa ini?

Do you have <u>a book</u>?
Kamu punya <u>buku</u>?

<u>The book</u> is on the table.
<u>Buku</u> di atas meja.

The Linking Verb ("to be")

There is no Indonesian equivalent for the English words "am," "is," "are" "was," and "were." The Indonesian equivalents of English sentences featuring conjugations of "to be" simply drop the word from the sentence. For example:

Ini buku.
This [is] a book.

Saya dokter.
I [am] a doctor.

Ibu sakit.
Mother [is] sick.

Kami pelajar.
We [are] students.

The Negative Sentence

The negative of a sentence equating nouns is formed by adding the word *bukan* before the second noun. For example:

Ini bukan buku.
This [is] not a book.

Saya bukan dokter.
I [am] not a doctor.

Kami bukan pelajar.
We [are] not students.

The negative of a descriptive sentence is formed by placing *tidak* before the adjective. For example:

Ibu tidak sakit.
Mother [is] not sick.

When forming the negative of subject-verb sentences, one precedes the verb with *tidak* as well. For example:

Ayah tidak datang.
Father did not come.

Saya tidak bisa pergi.
I cannot go.

The Interrogative Sentence

Interrogative sentences are formed one of three ways:

1. Adding a question mark. For example:

   Ibu sakit.   **Ibu sakit?**
   Mother is sick.   Is Mother sick?

   Ayah datang.   **Ayah datang?**
   Father came.   Did Father come?

2. Reversing the order of the subject and predicate and affixing the suffix *kah* to the word being emphasized. For example:

   Sakitkah ibu?
   Is Mother sick?

   Datangkah ayah?
   Did Father come?

3. Beginning the sentence with the words **Apa** or **Apakah**. For example:

   Apa ibu sakit?
   Is Mother sick?

   Apakah ayah datang?
   Did Father come?

Responses to Questions

In Indonesian, one often responds affirmatively to a question by repeating the emphasized word. The subject noun is often omitted. For example:

Q: **Ibu <u>sakit</u>?**
   Is Mother sick?
A: **<u>Sakit</u>.**
   She is sick. (*lit.* Sick.)

Q: **Ayah <u>datang</u>?**
   Did Father come?
A: **<u>Datang</u>.**
   He came. (*lit.* Came.)

Q: **Kamu <u>mengerti</u>?**
   Do you understand?
A: **<u>Mengerti</u>.**
   I understand. (*lit.* Understand.)

When a sentence employs the equivalent of an English auxiliary verb, one responds affirmatively by simply repeating the auxiliary. For example:

Q: **Adik <u>sudah</u> tidur?**
   Has Sister slept?
A: **<u>Sudah</u>.**
   She has. (*lit.* Has.)

Q: **Anda <u>bisa</u> datang?**
   <u>Can</u> you come?
A: **<u>Bisa</u>.**
   I can. (*lit.* Can.)

Q: **<u>Boleh</u> kami pergi?**
   May we go?
A: **<u>Boleh</u>.**
   You may. (*lit.* May.)

One may also respond to a question with the equivalent of "yes" and "no." In Indonesian, one always says *ya* for "yes." The words for "no" are *bukan* and *tidak*. When the emphasized word in the question is a noun, the appropriate word for "no" is *bukan*. With adjectives and verbs, it is *tidak*. For example:

Q: **Apa ini bukumu?**
   Is this your book?
A: **Ya.**
   Yes.
   > **Bukan.**
   > No.

Q: **Kamu sakit?**
   Are you sick?
A: **Ya.**
   Yes.
   > **Tidak.**
   > No.

With most questions featuring an auxiliary verb, one answers negatively with *tidak*. However, if the verb is *sudah*, the equivalent of the English "have" when used as an auxiliary, one replies with the word *belum*. For example:

Q: **Adik <u>sudah</u> tidur?**
   Has Sister slept?
A: **<u>Belum</u>.**
   She hasn't (*lit.* Hasn't.)

Sentence Word Order

There are no fixed rules in Indonesian word order. For example:

I come from America.
Saya datang dari Amerika. (*lit.* I come from America.)
Dari Amerika saya datang. (*lit.* From America I come.)

Hasan goes to Bandung.
Hasan pergi ke Bandung. (*lit.* Hasan goes to Bandung.)
Pergi ke Bandung Hasan. (*lit.* Goes to Bandung Hasan.)
Ke Bandung Hasan pergi. (*lit.* To Bandung Hasan goes.)

Who is this?
Siapa ini? (*lit.* Who is this?)
Ini siapa? (*lit.* This is who?)

Although there is no fixed word order, many English speakers are more comfortable using the Subject-Verb-Object order most favored by their language.

Word Order for Adjectives, Nouns, and Possessives

In Indonesian, adjectives, nouns, and possessives (when in the attributive form) come after the nouns they modify.

Adjectives:

<u>pretty</u> woman	**wanita <u>cantik</u>**
<u>big</u> house	**rumah <u>besar</u>**
<u>white</u> cat	**kucing <u>putih</u>**

(Note: One may also add the word *yang* before the adjective, for example: *wanita yang cantik*, *rumah yang besar*, and *kucing yang putih*.)

Nouns:

<u>car</u> door	**pintu <u>mobil</u>**
<u>house</u> key	**kunci <u>rumah</u>**
<u>language</u> teacher	**guru <u>bahasa</u>**

Possessives:

<u>my</u> book	**buku <u>saya</u>**
<u>John's</u> book	**buku <u>John</u>**
<u>Father's</u> book	**buku <u>ayah</u>**

Verb Conjugation and Tense

Indonesian verbs are not conjugated. For example:

Saya baca.
I read.

Dia baca.
He reads.

They also do not have tenses. The tense is indicated by the sentence context. Adverbs generally indicate when an activity is taking place. For example, the statement "*Ibu pergi*" means that Mother is leaving, but there is no context—one doesn't know if she has left, she's leaving now, or she will be leaving. However, add the phrase "*tadi malam*" ("last night"), so the statement becomes "*Ibu pergi tadi malam*" ("Mother left last night"). The action is clearly in the past tense.

Although there are auxiliary verb equivalents such as *sudah* and *belum* that seem to indicate tense, these words are more akin to adverbs. The closest English equivalent to *sudah* is "already." The closest equivalent to *belum* is "not yet."

To indicate action in the present in a manner akin to the present progressive tense (in English, the auxiliary + the main verb + the suffix *–ing*), one precedes the verb with the word *sedang*. For example:

We <u>are</u> study<u>ing</u>.
Kami <u>sedang</u> belajar.

I <u>am</u> eat<u>ing</u>.
Saya <u>sedang</u> makan.

Brother is sleep<u>ing</u>.
Adik <u>sedang</u> tidur.

To indicate action in the future, one precedes the verb with the words *akan*, *mau*, or *hendak*. For example:

We <u>will</u> see the show.
Kami <u>akan</u> melihat pertunjukan.

I <u>am going to</u> buy a dictionary.
Saya <u>mau</u> membeli kamus.

Father shall be going to America.
Ayah <u>hendak</u> pergi ke Amerika.

Basic Verbs and Verbs with Affixes

There are two types of verbs: basic verbs and verbs with affixes.

Some examples of basic verbs:

arrive	**sampai, tiba**
be born	**lahir**
come	**datang**
come home	**pulang**
die, go off	**mati**
eat	**makan**
enter	**masuk**
forget	**lupa**
go, leave	**pergi**
pass	**lewat**
return	**kembali**
shower or bathe	**mandi**
sit	**duduk**
sleep	**tidur**
stay	**tinggal**
wake up	**bangun**

Verbs with affixes come with a prefix, usually *me*, *ber*, or *meng*. For example:

masak (cook)	**memasak**
lari (run)	**berlari**
gali (dig)	**menggali**

In general, the affixes do not change the meaning of the verb. They simply provide a common alternative way of saying it. For example:

I <u>cook</u> rice.
Saya <u>masak</u> nasi.
Saya <u>memasak</u> nasi.

He <u>runs</u>.
Dia <u>lari</u>.
Dia <u>berlari</u>.

Sometimes the first letter of a word is deleted or changed when a prefix is added. The most common are words beginning with k, p, s, t. For example:

kancing (to button)	**mengancing**
panggil (to call)	**memanggil**
sapa (to put)	**menyapa**
taruh (to put)	**menaruh**

Note: Be careful not to add affixes to verbs in the basic group. It will confuse the meaning.

Pronouns

Subject, Object, and Attributive Possessive Pronouns

In Indonesian, subject, object, and attributive possessive pronouns are identical.

I, me, my	**saya, aku**
you, you, your (*inf.*)	**kamu**
you, you, your (*inf.*)	**engkau**
you, you, your (*form.*)	**anda**
you, you, your (*inf., to a man*)	**bapak**
you, you, your (*inf., to a woman*)	**ibu**
he/she, him/her, his/her	**dia, ia**
we, us, our	**kami**
we, us, our	**kita**
you, you, your (*inf. pl.*)	**kalian**
you, you, your (*form. pl.*)	**kamu sekalian**
you, you, your (*form. pl.*)	**anda sekalian**
they, them, their	**mereka**

The pronouns *engkau* and *kamu* (and their derivatives) are for familiar address and used when speaking to relatives and children. Use *bapak* when speaking to a man and *ibu* for women. For example:

Who are you? (*to a man*)
Bapak siapa?

Who are you? (*to a woman*)
Ibu siapa?

The pronoun *anda* and its derivatives are used in more formal address and may be used when speaking to anyone.

The pronoun *kami* is used in the first-person plural when the listener is excluded. For example, in the statement "*kami dari Amerika*" ("we are from America"), the "we" does not include the listener. In contrast, one uses the pronoun *kita* in the first-person plural when the listener is included, for example "*kita dari Amerika.*" Another example:

Let <u>us</u> go.
Mari <u>kita</u> pergi.

Predicative Possessive Pronouns

Predicative possessive pronouns, such as "mine," "yours," etc., are formed by adding the word *punya* to the attributive possessive pronoun. Although it may appear before or after the attributive pronoun, it generally comes before.

mine	**punya saya**
yours	**punya kamu**
hers/his	**punya dia**
ours	**punya kami**
ours	**punya kita**
yours *(pl.)*	**punya kalian**
theirs	**punya mereka**

Interrogative Pronouns

how	**bagaimana**
how many/much	**berapa**
what	**apa**
when	**kapan**
where (to)	**ke mana**
where from	**dari mana**
where is	**di mana**
which	**mana**
who	**siapa**
whose	**punya siapa**
why	**mengapa, kenapa**

The word *siapa* is used in place of *apa* when asking a person's name. For example:

> <u>What</u> is your name?
> **Siapa namanya?**

One also uses *berapa* when asking a telephone number or address. For example:

> <u>What's</u> your phone number?
> **Berapa nomor teleponya?**

The word *apa* may be used to ask for transportation. In these instances it is also used with words *pakai*, *naik*, or *dengan*. For example:

> How do I get there?
> **Naik apa?**

One uses *di mana* to indicate place or a position. For example:

> <u>Where</u> is the post office?
> **Di mana kantor pos?**

The interrogative *ke mana* asks about movement to a place.

> <u>Where</u> is Mother going?
> **Ke mana ibu pergi?**

Determiners

The adverbial determiners *amat, sangat, sekali* all mean "very." There is no difference between them. The words *amat* and *sangat* are placed before adjectives. For example:

| <u>very</u> pretty | **amat bagus** |
| <u>very</u> expensive | **sangat mahal** |

However, the word *sekali* always comes after the adjectives. For example:

| <u>very</u> pretty | **bagus <u>sekali</u>** |
| <u>very</u> expensive | **mahal <u>sekali</u>** |

Plural

In Indonesian, one generally indicates the plural by either repetition of adjectives or repetition of nouns. For example:

Indonesian women are <u>pretty</u>.
Wanita Indonesia <u>cantik-cantik</u>.

<u>Dresses</u> in the market are very cheap.
<u>Baju-baju</u> di pasar murah sekali.

If the plural is indicated by a number, determiner, or any other word, there is no repetition. For example:

I want <u>two pens</u>.
Saya mau <u>dua pena</u>.

There are <u>many cars</u> in the street.
Ada <u>banyak mobil</u> di jalan.

<u>All streets</u> are closed.
<u>Semua jalan</u> ditutup.

INDONESIAN–ENGLISH DICTIONARY

A

abad (*n*) century
abis (*adj*) (**habis**) no left over, gone
abjad (*n*) alphabet
abu (*n*) ash, dirt
abu-abu (*adj*) gray
a.c. (*n*) air conditioning
acak (*adj*) random
acak-acakan (*adj*) disarray, messy
acara (*n*) agenda, program (*TV, radio*)
ada (*v*) to have, to own, there is
ada apa (*adv*) what's the matter
ada kalanya (*adv*) sometimes, often
adat (*n*) custom, character
adat istiadat (*n*) custom and tradition
adik laki-laki (*n*) brother (*younger*)
adik perempuan (*n*) sister (*younger*)
adil (*adj*) justified, fair, just
aduk (*v*) (**mengaduk**) to stir
agak (*adv*) rather, somewhat
agaknya (*adv*) seem
agar supaya (*adv*) in order to, so
Agustus (*n*) August
ahli (*n*) expert, specialist
air (*n*) water, juice
air anggur (*n*) grape juice
air apel (*n*) apple juice
air jeruk (*n*) orange juice
air mata (*n*) tears
air minum (*n*) drinking water
air panas (*n*) hot water
air putih (*n*) water

air tomat (*n*) tomato juice
ajak (*v*) (**mengajak**) to invite
ajar (*v*) (**belajar**) to study; (**mengajar**) to teach
ajaran (*n*) teaching
akal (*n*) mind; **masuk akal** (*adj*) reasonable
akan (*v*) to want to, will, going to
akan datang (*adv*) next, the following
akhir (*n*) end
akhirnya (*adv*) finally
akibat (*n*) result
akta (*n*) certificate
akta kelahiran (*n*) birth certificate
aktif (*adj*) active
aktivis (*n*) activist
aktor (*n*) actor
aktris (*n*) actress
aku (*pron*) I (*familiar*)
akur (*adj*) harmonious, matching; (*v*) to get along,
        to match
alam (*n*) nature
alamat (*n*) address
alergi (*n*) allergy
alfabet (*n*) alphabet
alis (*n*) eyebrow
alis mata (*n*) eyebrow
alpokat (*n*) avocado
alun-alun (*n*) town square
alus (*adj*) (**halus**) soft, gentle
amal (*n*) charity, good deed
aman (*adj*) safe, secure, peaceful
amanat (*n*) speech
amat (*adv*) very
ambil (*v*) (**mengambil**) to take
ambisi (*n*) ambition
ambruk (*v*) to collapse
Amerika (*n*) America
ampas (*n*) garbage, waste
amplop (*n*) envelope
amuk (*n*) rampage; (*v*) (**mengamuk**) to run amok

anak (*n*) child
anak laki-laki (*n*) boy, son
anak muda (*n*) young people
anak orok (*n*) infant, baby
anak perempuan (*n*) daughter, girl
anak-anakan (*n*) doll
andaikata (*adv*) if, if only
andil (*n*) share
anggaran (*n*) budget
anggota (*n*) member
anggrek (*n*) orchid
anggun (*adj*) graceful
anggur (*n*) wine, grape
angin (*n*) wind
angin puyuh (*n*) typhoon
angin sepoi-sepoi (*n*) breeze
angin topan (*n*) tornado, hurricane
angka (*n*) number, statistic
angkasa (*n*) cloud
angkasawan (*n*) astronaut (*male*)
angkasawati (*n*) astronaut (*female*)
angkat (*v*) to adopt (*a child*); (**mengangkat**) to lift,
    to remove
angkatan (*n*) generation
angker (*adj*) haunted
angket (*n*) poll, survey
angkuh (*adj*) arrogant
angsa (*n*) goose
angus (*adj*) (**hangus**) burn
anjing (*n*) dog
anjuran (*n*) suggestion
antar (*v*) (**mengantar**) to drop off
antara (*prep*) between, amongst
antibiotik (*n*) antibiotic
antik (*n*) antique
antingan (*n*) earring
anting-anting (*n*) earring
antri (*v*) to stand in line
apa (*adv*) what

apa-apa (*adv*) everything
apal (*v*) to memorize
apel (*n*) apple
api (*n*) fire
apotek (*n*) drugstore, pharmacy
April (*n*) April
arah (*n*) direction
arak-arakan (*n*) parade
arsitek (*n*) architect
arti (*n*) meaning; (*v*) mean
artis (*n*) actress
arus (*n*) current
asal (*adj*) original; (*n*) origin
asam (*adj*) sour
asbak (*n*) ashtray
aseli (*adj*) original, genuine, authentic
asem (*adj*) sour
asin (*adj*) salty
asing (*adj*) unfamiliar
asli (*adj*) original, genuine, authentic
atap (*n*) roof
atas (*prep*) above, on, for; **atas nama** on behalf
atasan (*n*) superior
atau (*conj*) or
atlas (*n*) map, atlas
atur (*v*) (**mengatur**) to arrange, to regulate
aturan (*n*) rules, regulation
Australia (*n*) Australia
awan (*n*) cloud
ayah (*n*) father
ayam (*n*) chicken

B

bab (*n*) chapter
babak belur (*adj*) black and blue
babi (*n*) pig, pork
babi panggang (*n*) roasted pork

babu (*n*) servant
baca (*v*) (**membaca**) to read
bacaan (*n*) reading, literature
badan (*n*) body, committee
badminton (*n*) badminton
badut (*n*) clown
bagai (*adv*) (**bagaikan**) like, as
bagaimana (*adv*) how
bagi (*prep*) to, of; (*v*) (**membagi**) to divide
bagian (*n*) part
bagus (*adj*) good, pretty
bahan (*n*) ingredient, material
bahasa (*n*) language
bahasa Indonesia (*n*) Indonesian language
bahasa Inggris (*n*) English language
bahasa Jerman (*n*) German language
bahasa Perancis (*n*) French language
bahkan (*adv*) even
bahu (*n*) shoulder
baik (*adj*) (**baik-baik**) fine, good
baja (*n*) steel
bajak (*v*) (**membajak**) to hijack
baju (*n*) dress, clothes
baju blus (*n*) blouse
baju kaos (*n*) t-shirt
baju terusan (*n*) dress
baju tidur (*n*) nightgown
bakal (*adv*) will (*future*)
bakul (*n*) basket
balon (*n*) baloon
bambu (*n*) bamboo
bandel (*adj*) thick-headed
bangun (*v*) to wake up
bank (*n*) bank
bantah (*v*) (**membantah**) to deny
bantal (*n*) pillow
bantu (*v*) (**membantu**) to help
bantuan (*n*) help
bapak (*n*) father, sir, Mr.

bapak pendiri (*n*) founding father
barang (*n*) stuff, thing
barangkali (*adv*) maybe
bareng (*adv*) together
baris (*n*) line; (*v*) (**berbaris**) to march
baru (*adj*) new
baru saja (*adv*) just now
baru-baru ini (*adv*) recently
barusan (*adv*) just now
basah (*adj*) wet
batu es (*n*) ice cube
batuk (*n, v*) cough
bawang (*n*) onion
bawang putih (*n*) garlic
bayam (*n*) spinach
bea (*n*) fee
beban (*n*) burden, load
bebas (*adj*) free
bebek (*n*) duck
becak (*n*) rickshaw
becek (*adj*) muddy
beda (*adj*) different
bedah (*v*) to do surgery
bedak (*n*) powder
bedanya (*n*) difference
bedil (*n*) gun, pistol, bayonet
beha (*n*) bra
bekas istri (*n*) ex-wife
bekas suami (*n*) ex-husband
belajar (*v*) to study, to learn
Belanda (*n*) The Netherlands
beli (*v*) (**membeli**) to buy
belimbing (*n*) starfruit
beling (*n*) glass
belum (*adv*) not yet, haven't
belut (*n*) eel
benang (*n*) thread
bencana (*n*) disaster
benci (*v*) (**membenci**) to hate

benda (*n*) thing, material
bendera (*n*) flag
bengkak (*adj*) swollen
bengkel (*n*) garage
bensin (*n*) gasoline
bentuk (*n*) shape
berangkat (*v*) to leave, to depart
berapa (*pron*) what price, how much, how many
berapa banyak (*pron*) how much, how many
berapa lama (*pron*) how long
berapa orang (*pron*) how many people
beras (*n*) rice (*uncooked*)
berat (*adj*) heavy
berbuat (*v*) to commit
berbunyi (*v*) to sound
berdikari (*adj*) independent
berdiri (*v*) to stand up
berdoa (*v*) to pray
berdua (*adj, adv*) in a group of two
beres (*adj*) done, finished, tidy
berfungsi (*v*) to function
berguna (*adj*) useful
berhenti (*v*) to stop, to quit
berikut (*adj, adv*) following, next
berkata (*v*) to say
berkisar (*adv*) around, about
berkurang (*adj*) down; (*v*) to reduce
berlaku (*adj*) valid
bermacam-macam (*adj*) all kinds
bermalam (*v*) to spend the night
bermimpi (*v*) to dream
berminat (*v*) to intend, to interest
bersiap-siap (*v*) to get ready
bersih (*adj*) clean
berteman (*v*) to become friends with
bertemu (*v*) to meet
bertengkar (*v*) to fight, to argue
bertepuk tangan (*v*) to clap hands, to applaud
beruang (*n*) bear

berwajib (*n*) (**yang berwajib**) authority
berwarna (*adj*) colored
besar (*adj*) big, large, grand
besi (*n*) iron
besok (*adv, n*) tomorrow
besok lusa (*adv/n*) day after tomorrow
besuk (*v*) to visit (*someone in the hospital*)
betis (*n*) knee
bibi (*n*) aunt
bibir (*n*) lip
bicara (*v*) (**berbicara**) to speak
bidan (*n*) midwife
bilang (*v*) to say, to count
bilangan (*n*) number
bimbang (*adj*) uncertain
binatang (*n*) animal
binatang kesayangan (*n*) pet
bingkai (*n*) frame
bingkisan (*n*) gift, package
bingung (*adj*) confused
bintang (*n*) star
bintang film (*n*) movie star
bir (*n*) beer
biru (*adj*) blue
bisa (*adj*) able to; (*n*) poison
bising (*adj*) noisy
bisu (*adj*) deaf
blus (*n*) blouse
bocah (*n*) kid, child
bocor (*v*) to leak
bodoh (*adj*) foolish, stupid
bola voli (*n*) volleyball
boleh (*adv*) may; (*v*) to allow
bolong (*v*) to have hole(s)
bon (*n*) bill
bosan (*adj*) bored, boring
botak (*adj*) bald
botol (*n*) bottle
bros (*n*) pin

buah (*n*) (**buah-buahan**) fruit
buat (*prep*) for, to; (*v*) (**membuat**) to make
Budha (*n*) Buddhist
bujuk (*v*) (**membujuk**) to persuade
buka (*v*) open; (**membuka**) to open
bukan (*adv*) no, not (*before nouns*)
bukit (*n*) hill
bukti (*n*) evidence
buku (*n*) book
buku catatan (*n*) notebook
buku pedoman (*n*) guidebook
buku telepon (*n*) telephone book
bulan (*n*) moon, month
bulanan (*adj*) monthly
bulat (*adj*) round
bulu (*n*) feather, hair
buncis (*n*) green bean
bundar (*adj*) round
bunga (*n*) flower
bunga anggrek (*n*) orchid
bunga mawar (*n*) rose
bungkus (*v*) (**membungkus**) to wrap
bungsu (*adj*) youngest (*of a child*)
buntut (*n*) tail
bunyi (*n*) sound, noise
buram (*adj*) blurry
buruk (*adj*) ugly, bad
burung (*n*) bird
busuk (*adj*) rotten, bad smelling; (*n*) bad smell

C

cabai (*n*) chili pepper
cabe (*n*) chili pepper
cahaya (*n*) beam, light, glow
cair (*n*) liquid
cakap (*adj*) able, capable, handsome, beautiful
        (*describing a person*)

cakep (*adj*) handsome, beautiful (*describing a person*)
calon (*n*) future
calon istri (*n*) future wife
calon suami (*n*) future husband
campur (*v*) (**mencampur**) to mix
campur aduk (*v*) to mix up
candi (*n*) temple
candu (*n*) addiction
cangkir (*n*) cup
cantik (*adj*) pretty, beautiful (*describing a woman*)
cara (*n*) way, method
cari (*v*) (**mencari**) to look for
catat (*v*) (**mencatat**) to write
catatan (*n*) note(s)
catur (*n*) chess
celana (*n*) pants
celana dalam (*n*) underwear, panties
celana panjang (*n*) pants
celana pendek (*n*) shorts
celup (*v*) to dip
cemara (*n*) pine tree
cemburu (*adj*) jealous
cepat (*adj*) quick, fast
cerai (*adj*) divorced, separated
ceramah (*n*) speech; (*v*) to give a speech
cerewet (*adj*) fussy, talkative
cerita (*n*) story; (*v*) to tell
cerutu (*n*) cigar
cina (*n*) China, Chinese
cinta (*n*) love; (*v*) to love
cita-cita (*n*) dream; (*v*) to want to become
coba (*adv*) please; (*v*) (**mencoba**) to try, to attempt
coklat (*adj*) brown
conditioner (*n*) conditioner
contoh (*n*) example
corak (*n*) pattern
corong (*n*) funnel
cuaca (*n*) weather, climate
cucu (*n*) grandchild

cucu laki-laki (*n*) grandson
cucu perempuan (*n*) granddaughter
cuka (*n*) vinegar
cukup (*adj*) enough, adequate, sufficient, fit
cukur (*v*) (**bercukur**) to shave
cuma (*adv*) only, just
cuma-cuma (*adv*) free
cumi-cumi (*n*) squid
curam (*adj*) steep
curang (*adj*) shrewd
curi (*v*) (**mencuri**) to steal
curiga (*adj*) suspicious
cuti (*n, v*) leave
cuti hamil (*n*) maternity leave

D

dada (*n*) chest, breast
daftar makanan (*n*) menu
dagang (*v*) (**berdagang**) to sell, to trade
daging (*n*) meat
dagu (*n*) chin
dahan (*n*) tree
dahsyat (*adj*) extraordinary
dalam (*adj*) deep; (*prep*) inside
damai (*adj*) peaceful
dana (*n*) fund
dansa (*n*) dance; (*v*) (**berdansa**) to dance
dapat (*adj*) able to
dapur (*n*) kitchen
dari (*prep*) from
dari mana (*prep*) where from
darurat (*adj*) emergency
dasar (*n*) foundation, base
dasi (*n*) tie
dasi kupu-kupu (*n*) necktie
data (*n*) data
datang (*v*) to come

daun (*n*) leaf
daun bawang (*n*) green onion
daya upaya (*n*) effort
dekat (*prep*) near, nearby
delapan (*num*) eight
delapan belas (*num*) eighteen
delapan puluh (*num*) eighty
demam (*n*) fever
dengan (*prep*) with, by
dengar (*v*) (**mendengar**) to hear, to listen
deodoran (*n*) deodorant
depan (*prep*) in front
desa (*n*) village
desak (*v*) (**mendesak**) to urge, to put pressure
Desember (*n*) December
detik (*n*) second
dia (*pron*) he, she
diam (*adj*) silent; (*v*) (**berdiam**) to stay, to live
dingin (*adj*) cold
diplomat (*n*) diplomat
dokter (*n*) doctor
dokter gigi (*n*) dentist
dolar (*n*) dollar
domba (*n*) lamb
dompet (*n*) bag, wallet
dua (*num*) two
dua belas (*num*) twelve
dua kali (*adv*) twice
dua puluh (*num*) twenty
dua ratus (*num*) two hundred
duduk (*v*) to sit
dukun (*n*) paranormal
dulu (*adj*) former; (*adv*) in the past
dunia (*n*) world
duri (*n*) thorn
durian (*n*) durian (*fruit*)
dusun (*n*) village
duta (*n*) representative
duta besar (*n*) ambassador

E

edan (*adj*) crazy
edaran (*n*) leaflet
edisi (*n*) edition
editor (*n*) editor
edukasi (*n*) education
eja (*v*) (**mengeja**) to spell
ejaan (*n*) spelling
ejek (*v*) (**mengejek**) to ridicule
ekor (*n*) tail
elit (*n*) elite
embun (*n*) dew
emosi (*adj*) emotional; (*n*) emotion
empat (*num*) four
empat belas (*num*) fourteen
empat puluh (*num*) forty
enam (*num*) six
enam belas (*num*) sixteen
enam puluh (*num*) sixty
encer (*adj*) watery
enggan (*adj*) reluctant, unwilling
entahlah (*adv*) don't know
enteng (*adj*) light
Eropa (*n*) Europe
es (*n*) ice
es batu (*n*) ice cube
es krim (*n*) ice cream
evakuasi (*n*) evacuation; (*v*) (**mengevakuasi**) to
        evacuate
evaluasi (*n*) evaluation; (*v*) (**mengevaluasi**) to evaluate
evolusi (*n*) evolution

F

fajar (*n*) dawn
fakta (*n*) fact
faktor (*n*) factor

fakultas (*n*) faculty
falsafah (*n*) philosophy
famili (*n*) relatives
farmasi (*n*) pharmacy
Februari (*n*) February
film (*n*) film
filosofi (*n*) philosophy
filter (*n*) filter
firasat (*n*) instinct, feeling
firma (*n*) firm
flu (*n*) influenza
forum (*n*) forum
foto (*n*) photograph
fotokopi (*n*) photocopy
fungsi (*n*) function

G

gabung (*v*) (**bergabung**) to unite, to combine
gading (*n*) tusk
gadis (*n*) maiden, young girl
gajah (*n*) elephant
gaji (*n*) earnings, wages
gali (*v*) to dig
gambar (*n*) (**gambaran**) picture, photo, image
game (*n*) game
gampang (*adj*) easy
ganja (*n*) marijuana
ganteng (*adj*) handsome
ganti (*v*) (**mengganti**) to change, to substitute, to replace
gantian (*v*) (**bergantian**) to take turns
gantung (*v*) (**menggantung**) to hang; (**tergantung**) to
    depend on
gantungan baju (*n*) clothes hanger
gantungan handuk (*n*) towel rack
garam (*n*) salt
garis (*n*) line
garpu (*n*) fork

garuk (*v*) (**menggaruk**) to scratch
gatal (*adj*) itchy; (*n*) itch
gawat (*adj*) urgent, dangerous
gelang (*n*) bracelet
gelang karet (*n*) rubber band
gelap (*adj*) dark
gelas (*n*) glass
gemar (*v*) to like
gembala (*n*) shepherd
gembira (*adj*) glad, happy
gempa (*n*) earthquake
gempa bumi (*n*) earthquake
gendut (*adj*) fat (*describing a person*)
genteng (*n*) roof
gepeng (*adj*) thin
gerak (*v*) (**bergerak**) to move
gereja (*n*) church
gesit (*adj*) agile, works fast, moves fast
gigi (*n*) tooth
gila (*adj*) mad, crazy
giliran (*n*) turn
ginjal (*n*) kidney
girang (*adj*) happy, glad
gorden (*n*) curtain
goreng (*v*) to fry
gosip (*n*) gossip
gosok gigi (*v*) (**menggosok gigi**) to brush one's teeth
gratis (*adj*) free, gratis
gua (*n*) cave
gubuk (*n*) hut
gudang (*n*) storage, warehouse
gula (*n*) sugar
gula-gula (*n*) candy
gulai (*n*) curry
gulat (*n*) wrestling
gulung (*v*) to roll
gunanya (*n*) use
gunting (*n*) scissors; (*v*) (**menggunting**) to cut
gunting kuku (*n*) nail clipper

gunung (*n*) mountain
gunung berapi (*n*) volcano
gurih (*adj*) delicious
guru (*n*) teacher
gurun pasir (*n*) desert
gusi (*n*) gum

H

habis (*adj*) gone
hakim (*n*) judge
halo (*interj*) hello
hambar (*adj*) tasteless
hambur (*adj*) wasted
hampir (*adv*) almost, nearly
handuk (*n*) towel
hantu (*n*) ghost, spirit
hanya (*adv*) only
hapus (*v*) (**menghapus**) to abolish, to erase
harapan (*n*) hope
hari (*n*) day
hari ini (*adv*) today
harian (*adj*) daily
harus (*v*) must
hati (*n*) liver
hati-hati (*adj*) careful; (*v*) to beware
haus (*adj*) thirsty
hawa (*n*) weather, climate
heran (*adj*) bewildered
hiasan (*n*) decoration
hidangan (*n*) meal, food
hidung (*n*) nose
hidup (*adj*) alive; (*n*) life; (*v*) to be alive, to live
hijau (*adj*) green
hilang (*adj*) lost, stolen, gone; (*v*) to lose, to steal
Hindu (*n*) Hindu
hingga (*adv*) till, until
hitam (*adj*) black

hitam putih (*adj*) black-and-white
hitung (*v*) (**menghitung, berhitung**) to count
hormat (*n*) respect
hotel (*n*) hotel
hubung (*v*) (**menghubungi**) to contact
hujan (*n*) rain
hukum (*n*) law; (*v*) (**menghukum**) to punish
hutan (*n*) forest
hutang (*n*) debt; (*v*) (**berhutang**) to owe

I

ia (*pron*) he, she
ibu (*n*) mother, madame, Mrs.
ibu kota (*n*) capital city
ibu negara (*n*) First Lady
ijazah (*n*) diploma
ikan (*n*) fish, meat
ikat (*v*) (**mengikat**) to bind, to tie
ikat pinggang (*n*) belt
ikhtiar (*n*) pledge; (*v*) (**berikhtiar**) to pledge
ikut (*v*) to follow, to come along
ilmu (*n*) knowledge, science
ilmuwan (*n*) scientist
ilustrasi (*n*) illustration
imbalan (*n*) reward
imigrasi (*n*) immigration
imitasi (*n*) imitation, fake
impian (*n*) dream, hope
impor (*n*) import; (*v*) (**mengimpor**) to import
imunisasi (*n*) immunization
indah (*adj*) beautiful, pretty
individu (*n*) individual
induk (*n*) mother
infeksi (*n*) infection
influenza (*n*) influenza
ingat (*v*) to remember
ingatan (*n*) memory, mind

Inggris (*n*) England
ingin (*v*) to wish, want to
ini (*pron*) this
inisiatif (*n*) initiative
injak (*v*) (**menginjak**) to step
insinyur (*n*) engineer
irama (*n*) tune, rhythm
iri (*adj*) jealous
iri hati (*adj*) jealous
iris (*v*) (**mengiris**) to slice, to chop
irisan (*n*) slice
irit (*v*) (**mengirit**) to save, to economize
Islam (*n*) Moslem
istri (*n*) wife
itik (*n*) duck
itu (*pron*) that
itung (*v*) to count
iya (*adv*) yes
izin (*n*) permission

J

jadi (*adv*) so; (*v*) to become
jadwal (*n*) schedule
jagung (*n*) corn
jaket (*n*) jacket
jalan (*n*) street
jam (*n*) hour
jam dinding (*n*) clock
jam tangan (*n*) watch
jaman (*n*) era, time
jamin (*v*) (**menjamin**) to guarantee
jaminan (*n*) warranty
jamu (*n*) herb
jamur (*n*) mushroom
janda (*n*) widow
janji (*n*) date, promise; (*v*) (**berjanji**) to promise
jantung (*n*) heart

jantung hati (*n*) sweetheart
Januari (*n*) January
jarak (*n*) distance
jarang (*adv*) seldom, rarely
jari (*n*) finger
jari kaki (*n*) toe
jarum (*n*) needle
jas (*n*) suit
jatuh (*v*) to fall
jatuh sakit (*v*) to fall ill
jejak (*n*) step
jejaka (*n*) bachelor
jelas (*adj*) clear
jelek (*adj*) ugly, bad
jembatan (*n*) bridge
jempol (*n*) thumb
jemput (*v*) (**menjemput**) to pick up
jemu (*adj*) bored, boring
jemur (*v*) (**menjemur**) to air, to dry
jemuran (*n*) laundry
jendela (*n*) window
jerawat (*n*) pimple
Jerman (*n*) Germany
jeruk (*n*) orange
jika (*conj*) if
jiwa (*n*) life, soul
jodoh (*n*) soul mate
jorok (*adj*) dirty
jual (*v*) (**menjual**) to sell
jualan (*n*) sale
juara (*n*) champion
judi (*v*) (**berjudi**) to gamble
judul (*n*) title
juga (*adv*) also
jujur (*adj*) honest
Juli (*n*) July
Jumat (*n*) Friday
jumpa (*v*) (**berjumpa**) to meet
Juni (*n*) June

jurang (*n*) ravine
juri (*n*) jury
juru ketik (*n*) typist
jururawat (*n*) nurse
jutaan (*n*) million
jutawan (*n*) millionaire

K

kabar (*n*) news
kabur (*adj*) blurry; (*v*) to run away
kabut (*n*) fog, mist
kaca (*n*) mirror
kacang (*n*) nut, peanut
kacang polong (*n*) pea(s)
kadang kala (*adv*) often
kadang-kadang (*adv*) sometimes, occasionally
kain (*n*) cloth
kakak (*n*) older brother, older sister
kakak laki-laki (*n*) brother (*older*)
kakak perempuan (*n*) sister (*older*)
kakek (*n*) grandfather
kaki (*n*) leg
kaku (*adj*) awkward, stiff
kalah (*v*) to lose
kalau (*conj*) if
kalau-kalau (*adv*) just in case
kaleng (*n*) tin
kali (*n*) ditch, time(s); **dua kali** (*adv*) twice; **satu kali**
     (*adv*) once
kalian (*pron*) all of you
kalimat (*n*) sentence
kalkulator (*n*) calculator
kalung (*n*) necklace
kamar (*n*) room, chamber
kamar kecil (*n*) bathroom
kamar mandi (*n*) bathroom
Kamis (*n*) Thursday

kampanye (*n*) campaign
kampung (*n*) village
kampus (*n*) campus
kamus (*n*) dictionary
Kanada (*n*) Canada
kanan (*n*) right
kancing (*n*) button; (*v*) (**mengancing**) to button
kandang (*n*) cage
kantin (*n*) canteen
kantong (*n*) pocket
kantor (*n*) office
kantor imigrasi (*n*) immigration office
kantor polisi (*n*) police station
kantor pos (*n*) post office
kantor telepon (*n*) telephone office
kantor turis (*n*) tourist office
kantung (*n*) pocket
kaos (*n*) t-shirt
kaos kaki (*n*) sock(s)
kapal (*n*) ship
kapan (*adv*) when
kapan saja (*adv*) whenever
kapas (*n*) cotton
kapur (*n*) chalk
kartu (*n*) card
kartu pos (*n*) postcard
karuan (*adj*) decent
karung (*n*) sack
kasar (*adj*) rude, rough
kasih (*v*) to give
kasih tahu (*v*) to inform, to report
kasihan (*v*) to feel sorry
kasir (*n*) cashier
kasur (*n*) mattress
kasut (*n*) sandal
kata (*n*) word
katak (*n*) toad, frog
Katolik (*n*) Catholic, Roman Catholic
kawan (*n*) friend

kawin (*v*) to marry
kaya (*adj*) rich
kaya raya (*adj*) very rich
kayu (*n*) wood
kebal (*adj*) immune
kebanyakan (*n*) most of, majority
keberanian (*n*) bravery, courage
keberatan (*v*) to mind
kebiasaan (*n*) habit
kebingungan (*adj*) confused; (*n*) confusion
kebun (*n*) garden
kebutuhan (*n*) need, necessity
kecambah (*n*) bean sprouts
kecewa (*adj*) disappointed
kecil (*adj*) small
kedai (*n*) shop
kedudukan (*n*) position
kedutaan (*n*) embassy
kegemaran (*n*) hobby
keibuan (*adj*) maternal
keindahan (*n*) beauty
kejam (*adj*) cruel
keju (*n*) cheese
kejutan (*n*) surprise
kekejaman (*n*) cruelty, brutality
kekeliruan (*n*) mistake, fault
kekuasaan (*n*) power
kekuatan (*n*) strength
kekurangan (*n*) disadvantage, flaw, shortage
kelabu (*adj*) gray
kelakuan (*n*) conduct
kelambu (*n*) mosquito net
kelaparan (*n*) hunger
kelar (*adj*) finished, completed
kelas (*n*) class, rank
kelebihan (*n*) advantage, surplus
kelelawar (*n*) bat
kelinci (*n*) rabbit
keluar (*v*) to go out, to exit

keluar negeri (*v*) to go abroad
keluhan (*n*) complaint
kemampuan (*n*) ability
kemarau (*n*) dry season
kemarin (*adv*) yesterday
kemauan (*n*) willingness, desire
kembali (*interj*) you're welcome; (*v*) to return
kembalian (*n*) change
kembang (*n*) flower
kembang api (*n*) fireworks
kembang kol (*n*) cauliflower
kembar (*n*) twins
kemeja (*n*) shirt
kemudian (*adv*) afterwards, later
kemungkinan (*n*) possibility
kenal (*v*) to know
kenalan (*n*) acquaintance, friend
kenapa (*pron*) why
kening (*n*) forehead
kental (*adj*) thick
kentang (*n*) potato
kenyang (*adj*) full
keong (*n*) snail
kepagian (*adv*) early
kepala (*n*) head
kepiting (*n*) crab
kepulauan (*n*) archipelago, island(s)
keputusan (*n*) decision
kerah (*n*) collar
keran (*n*) faucet
keranjang (*n*) basket
keras (*adj*) tough, hard; (*adv*) aloud
kering (*adj*) dry
keris (*n*) dagger
kerja (*v*) (**bekerja**) to work
kerjaan (*n*) work
kertas (*n*) paper
kertas tisu (*n*) tissue paper
kerut (*v*) (**mengerut**) to shrink

kesal (*adj*) annoyed, tired
kesan (*n*) impression
kesel (*adj*) annoyed, tired
keselamatan (*n*) safety
kesempatan (*n*) opportunity
kesudahan (*n*) aftermath
kesukaan (*n*) like
kesukaran (*n*) difficulty, hardship
ketabahan (*n*) patience, endurance
ketahuan (*v*) to be caught in
ketemu (*v*) to be found, to meet
keterangan (*n*) information, explanation
ketimun (*n*) cucumber
ketua (*n*) chief, director
ketuk (*v*) (**mengetuk**) to knock
kidal (*adj*) left-handed
kilat (*n*) lightning, express
kilo (*n*) kilogram, kilometer
kira (*v*) (**mengira**) to think, to assume
kira-kira (*adv*) about
kiri (*n*) left
kirim (*v*) (**mengirim**) to send
kisah (*n*) story
kita (*pron*) we
kocok (*v*) (**mengocok**) to shake
kode (*n*) code
kodok (*n*) frog
kol (*n*) cabbage
kolonye (*n*) cologne
komisi (*n*) commission
konsulat (*n*) consulate
kontan (*n*) cash
koran (*n*) newspaper
korek api (*n*) match(es)
kosong (*adj*) empty, blank
kota (*n*) city, town
kotak (*n*) box
kotak surat (*n*) mailbox
kotor (*adj*) dirty, soiled

Kristen (*n*) Christian
kuah (*n*) water, soup, gravy
kuat (*adj*) strong
kubis (*n*) cabbage
kue-kue (*n*) cake
kulit (*n*) skin
kuning (*adj*) yellow
kupas (*v*) (**mengupas**) to peel
kuping (*n*) ear
kurang (*adj*) less, lacking; (*v*) minus
kurang ajar (*adj*) disrespectful, impolite, rude
kurang lebih (*adv*) about, around
kurs (*n*) exchange rate
kurung (*v*) (**mengurung**) to lock up
kurus (*adj*) thin, lean
kusut (*n*) wrinkle
kutang (*n*) bra
kutek (*n*) nail polish

L

laba (*n*) profit
labu (*n*) pumpkin
lada (*n*) pepper
lagi (*adv*) more, again, back
lagi pula (*adv*) moreover, in addition
lagu (*n*) song
lahir (*v*) to be born
lain (*adj*) different, another
lain kali (*adv*) next time
lain lagi (*adv*) differently
lain waktu (*adv*) next time
laki (*n*) husband
laki-laki (*n*) male, man
laku (*v*) to sell, to sell out
lalat (*n*) fly (*insect*)
lalu (*adv*) then; (*v*) (**melalui**) to pass
lalu lintas (*n*) traffic

lama (*adj*) long, old
lambat (*adj*) slow
lampu (*n*) light, lamp
lantai (*n*) floor
lantas (*adv*) then
lapar (*adj*) hungry
lapis (*n*) layer
lari (*v*) (**berlari**) to run
laris (*v*) to sell out
latih (*v*) (**berlatih**) to practice; (**melatih**) to train
latihan (*n*) training, practice
laut (*n*) sea, ocean
lawan (*adv*) against
layang-layang (*n*) kite
lebah (*n*) bee
lebar (*adj*) wide
lebat (*adj*) heavy
lebih (*adj*) more
lebih besar (*adj*) bigger
lebih suka (*v*) to prefer
legenda (*n*) legend, myth
leher (*n*) neck
lem (*n*) glue
lembab (*adj*) humid
lembah (*n*) valley
lembut (*adj*) tender
lempar (*v*) (**melempar**) to throw
lengan (*n*) arm, sleeve
lensa (*n*) lens
letak (*n*) location
lewat (*v*) to pass
liar (*adj*) wild, loose
libur (*adj*) off; (*v*) (**berlibur**) to be on vacation
liburan (*n*) vacation
licik (*adj*) shrewd, cunning, sly
licin (*adj*) slippery
lidah (*n*) tongue
lihat (*v*) (**melihat**) to see
lima (*num*) five

lima belas (*num*) fifteen
lima puluh (*num*) fifty
lingkaran (*n*) circle
lipstik (*n*) lipstick
loket (*n*) window
lomba (*v*) (**berlomba**) to race
longgar (*adj*) loose
lotion (*n*) lotion
luas (*adj*) large
lubang (*n*) hole
luka (*adj*) hurt, injured; (*n*) wound
lukis (*v*) (**melukis**) to draw, to paint (*a picture, etc.*)
lukisan (*n*) painting, drawing
lumayan (*adj*) moderate
lumpuh (*adj*) lame
lumpur (*n*) mud
lupa (*v*) to forget
lusa (*n*) day after tomorrow

M

maaf (*adj*) sorry (*I'm sorry*), (*v*) excuse me
mabuk (*adj*) drunk
madu (*n*) honey
mahal (*adj*) expensive, costly
mahasiswa (*n*) student
mahir (*adj*) skilled, talented
main (*v*) (**bermain**) to play
main-main (*adj*) not serious; (*v*) to joke, to kid around
majalah (*n*) magazine
maju (*adj*) advanced, developing; (*v*) to progress,
    to advance
maka (*adv*) so, then
makan (*v*) to eat
makan waktu (*v*) to take time
makanan (*n*) food
makanan kaleng (*n*) canned food
makin (*adv*) more
maklum (*v*) to understand

makmur (*adj*) prosperous
mal (*n*) mall
malah (*adv*) even
malahan (*adv*) even
malam (*n*) evening, night
malam ini (*adv*) tonight
malas (*adj*) lazy
maling (*v*) to steal
malu (*adj*) ashamed, shy, bashful
mama, mamak (*n*) mother, mama
mampir (*v*) to stop by, to visit
mampu (*adj*) capable, well-to-do
mana (*pron*) where, which
mandi (*v*) to take a bath, to take a shower
mandiri (*adj*) independent
mangga (*n*) mango
manggis (*n*) mangosteen
mangkok (*n*) bowl
mantap (*adj*) stable
mantu laki-laki (*n*) son-in-law
mantu perempuan (*n*) daughter-in-law
manusia (*n*) man, mankind, human
mapan (*adj*) stable
marah (*adj*) angry
Maret (*n*) March
margarin (*n*) margarine
mari (*interj*) bye, good-bye, let's; **mari kita pergi** let's go
masa (*adv*) really
masak (*adj*) ripe; (*v*) (**memasak**) to cook
masak air (*v*) to boil water
masakan (*n*) food, cooking
maskara (*n*) mascara
masuk (*v*) to enter
masuk akal (*adj*) reasonable
mata (*n*) eye
mata uang (*n*) currency
matahari (*n*) sun
mata-mata (*n*) spy
matang (*adj*) mature

mati (*adj*) dead, off, not working, not running; (*v*) to die
mau (*adj*) willing; (*v*) to want, going to
megah (*adj*) big, great
Mei (*n*) May
meja (*n*) table
menang (*v*) to win
menari (*v*) to dance
mengapa (*pron*) why
mentah (*adj*) raw
mentega (*n*) butter
menu (*n*) menu
merah (*adj*) red
merah muda (*adj*) pink
merdeka (*adj*) free
merica (*n*) pepper
mertua laki-laki (*n*) father-in-law
mertua perempuan (*n*) mother-in-law
mesin (*n*) machine, engine
mesin cuci (*n*) washing machine
mesin jahit (*n*) sewing machine
mewah (*adj*) luxurious
mimpi (*n*) dream; (*v*) (**bermimpi**) to dream
Minggu (*n*) Sunday
mingguan (*adj*) weekly
minta (*v*) to ask, to request
minum (*v*) to drink
minuman (*n*) drink, beverage
minyak (*n*) oil, grease
minyak wangi (*n*) perfume
mirip (*adj*) resemble
misi (*n*) mission
miskin (*adj*) poor, needy
mistar (*n*) ruler
modal (*n*) capital
model (*n*) model
modern (*adj*) modern
moga-moga (*adv*) hopefully
mogok (*v*) to stop, to strike
montir (*n*) mechanic

monyet (*n*) monkey
moralitas (*n*) morality
motif (*n*) motive
motivasi (*n*) motivation
mual (*adj*) nauseous, sick
muat (*v*) to fit (*as with clothes, etc.*)
muda (*adj*) young, light
mudah (*adj*) easy
mujur (*adj*) fortunate
muka (*n*) face
mulai (*v*) to begin
mulia (*adj*) holy, sacred, noble
mulus (*adj*) smooth
mulut (*n*) mouth
munafik (*adj*) hypocritical; (*n*) hypocrite
mungkin (*adv*) probably, perhaps
murah (*adj*) cheap
murid (*n*) pupil, student
murni (*adj*) pure
museum (*n*) museum
musik (*n*) music
musikus (*n*) musician
musim (*n*) season
musim dingin (*n*) winter
musim gugur (*n*) fall, autumn
musim kemarau (*n*) dry season
musim panas (*n*) summer
musim penghujan (*n*) rainy season
musim salju (*n*) winter
musim semi (*n*) spring
musnah (*v*) to destroy
mustahil (*adj*) impossible
musti (*adv*) must
musuh (*n*) enemy
mutakhir (*adj*) modern
mutiara (*n*) pearl
mutlak (*adj*) absolute
mutu (*n*) quality
mutung (*adj*) burnt

N

nafas (*n*) breath; (*v*) (**bernafas**) to breathe
nafsu makan (*n*) appetite
nakal (*adj*) mischievous
nama (*n*) name
nanti (*adv*) later
nasi (*n*) rice (*cooked*)
nasib (*n*) fate, destiny
nasihat (*n*) advice
nasional (*adj*) national
naskah (*n*) manuscript
negara (*n*) country
negarawan (*n*) statesman
negeri (*n*) country
nekat (*adj*) brave, risk-taking
nelayan (*n*) fisherman
nenek (*n*) grandmother
neraca (*n*) balance, scale
netral (*adj*) neutral
ngobrol (*v*) to chat
ngomong (*v*) to say
niat (*n*) wish, intention; (*v*) (**berniat**) to intend
nikah (*v*) (**menikah**) to marry
nilai (*n*) value
nol (*num*) zero
nomor (*n*) number
nonton (*v*) (**menonton**) to see, to watch (*a movie, etc.*)
Nopember (*n*) November
Nota (*n*) bill
notaris (*n*) notary
nuklir (*adj*) nuclear
nyaman (*adj*) pleasant
nyanyi (*v*) (**bernyanyi**) to sing
nyanyian (*n*) song
nyaring (*adj*) clear (*describing a sound*)
nyaris (*adv*) nearly, almost
nyasar (*v*) to get lost

nyata (*adj*) real
nyatanya (*adv*) in reality
nyawa (*n*) soul, life
nyenyak (*adv*) soundly (*as with sleeping*)
nyonya (*n*) madam

O

obat (*n*) medicine
obat batuk (*n*) cough medicine
obat tidur (*n*) sleeping pill
obyek (*n*) object
odol (*n*) toothpaste
Oktober (*n*) October
olah raga (*n*) sport
oleh (*adv, prep*) by
oleh-oleh (*n*) souvenir, gift
oli (*n*) oil
ombak (*n*) wave
ompong (*adj*) toothless
ongkos (*n*) expense
operasi (*n*) operation; (*v*) (**mengoperasi**) to operate
optik (*adj*) optical
optimis (*n*) optimist
orang (*n*) person, people, man, woman
orang Amerika (*n*) American (*person*)
orang asing (*n*) foreigner
orang Australi(a) (*n*) Australian (*person*)
orang baru (*n*) newcomer
orang Belanda (*n*) Dutch (*person*)
orang Eropa (*n*) European (*person*)
orang Inggris (*n*) British (*person*)
orang Jerman (*n*) German (*person*)
orang Kanada (*n*) Canadian (*person*)
orang kaya (*n*) well-to-do
orang laki-laki (*n*) man
orang Perancis (*n*) French (*person*)
orang perempuan (*n*) woman

orang tua (*n*) parents, old people
oranye (*adj*) orange
organisasi (*n*) organization
orisinil (*adj*) original
orok (*n*) infant, baby
otak (*n*) brain
otot (*n*) muscle

P

pabean (*n*) customs house
pabrik (*n*) factory
pacar (*n*) girlfriend, boyfriend
pada (*prep*) on
padang (*n*) field, plain
padi (*n*) paddy
pagar (*n*) fence
pagi (*n*) morning
pagi tadi (*adv*) this morning
pagi-pagi (*adv*) early morning
pahit (*adj*) bitter
pajak (*n*) tax
pakai (*adv*) by, with; (*v*) (**memakai**) to wear, to put on
pakaian (*n*) clothes
paket (*n*) package, parcel; (*v*) (**memaket**) to send a
    package, to send a parcel
pala (*n*) nutmeg
palsu (*n*) fake, imitation
paman (*n*) uncle
pamer (*v*) (**memamerkan**) to show off, to exhibit
pameran (*n*) exhibit, exhibition
pamit (*v*) (**berpamitan**) to say good-bye
pandai (*adj*) clever, smart
pandangan (*n*) view
panggang (*adj*) roasted, baked; (*v*) (**memanggang**) to
    roast, to bake
panggil (*v*) (**memanggil**) to call, to summon
panggung (*n*) stage

panjang (*adj*) long
panjat (*v*) (**memanjat**) to climb
panjat doa (*v*) to pray
pantai (*n*) beach, shore
pantas (*adj*) proper
papa (*n*) father
parfum (*n*) perfume
parit (*n*) ditch
paru-paru (*n*) lung
pas (*adj*) fit
pasang (*n*) pair; (*v*) (**memasang**) to install
pasangan (*n*) couple
pasar (*n*) market
pasir (*n*) sand
paspor (*n*) passport
pasta gigi (*n*) toothpaste
pasti (*adj*) certain; (*adv*) certainly; (*v*) must, have to
pasukan (*n*) troops, soldier
patah (*adj*) broken; (*v*) to break
patung (*n*) statue
paus (*n*) pope
pawai (*n*) parade
payung (*n*) umbrella
pecah (*adj*) broken; (*v*) to break
pecin (*n*) monosodium
pedas (*adj*) hot, spicy
pedoman (*n*) guide, example
peduli (*v*) to care
pegangan (*n*) handle, guide
pegawai (*n*) worker, employee
pegawai pabrik (*n*) factory worker
pegawai pemerintah (*n*) government worker
pejalan kaki (*n*) pedestrian
pekerja (*n*) worker
pekerja kantor (*n*) office employee
pekerjaan (*n*) work, job
pekik (*v*) (**memekik**) to scream, to yell
pelabuhan (*n*) harbor
pelabuhan udara (*n*) airport

pelan (*adj*) (**pelan-pelan**) slow
pelangi (*n*) rainbow
pelaut (*n*) sailor
pelayan (*n*) waitress, waiter, shop assistant
pelihara (*v*) (**memelihara**) to take care
pelupa (*adj*) forgetful
pemakai (*n*) user
pemakaian (*n*) usage, use
pemalu (*n*) shy person
pemandangan (*n*) landscape, scenery
pembaca (*n*) reader
pembajak (*n*) hijacker
pembajakan (*n*) hijacking
pembantu (*n*) servant, helper
pembeli (*n*) buyer
pemberian (*n*) gift, present
pembukaan (*n*) opening
pemeliharaan (*n*) care
pemeriksaan (*n*) examination, search
pemerintah (*n*) government
pemilik (*n*) owner
peminta (*n*) (**peminta-minta**) beggar
pemondokan (*n*) lodging, accommodation
pemuda (*n*) young man
pemudi (*n*) young woman
pemukiman (*n*) residence
pena (*n*) pen
penanggalan (*n*) calendar
penata rambut (*n*) hairdresser
pendapat (*n*) point of view, opinion
pendapatan (*n*) earnings, wages
pendek (*adj*) short, brief
pendeta (*n*) priest
penerangan turis (*n*) tourist information
pengacara (*n*) lawyer
pengalaman (*n*) experience
pengantin (*n*) bride
pengantin laki-laki (*n*) bridegroom
pengarang (*n*) writer

pengarang buku (*n*) author
pengaruh (*n*) influence
penggaris (*n*) ruler
penggemar (*n*) fans
penglihatan (*n*) sight
pengungsi (*n*) refugee
pengunjung (*n*) visitor
pengusaha (*n*) businessman
pening (*adj*) dizzy
peninggalan (*n*) remnants, ruins
peniti (*n*) pin, safety pin
penjahit (*n*) tailor, seamstress
pensil (*n*) pencil
pensiun (*adj*) retired; (*n*) pension
penting (*adj*) important
penuh (*adj*) full
penulis (*n*) writer
penuntun (*n*) guide
penyakit (*n*) illness, disease
penyanyi (*n*) singer
penyebab (*n*) cause
pepaya (*n*) papaya
Perancis (*n*) France
perang (*n*) war
perangko (*n*) stamp
perasaan (*n*) feeling
peraturan (*n*) rules, regulation
perawan (*n*) virgin
perawat (*n*) nurse
perawatan (*n*) care
perbedaan (*n*) difference
perbuatan (*n*) act, action
perempuan (*n*) woman
pergi (*v*) to go, to leave
perhatian (*n*) attention
perhiasan (*n*) jewelry
periksa (*v*) (**memeriksa**) to check, to examine
perintah (*n*) order, command
perjaka (*n*) bachelor

perkara (*n*) issue, affair
perkawinan (*n*) marriage
perkiraan (*n*) estimate, calculation, assumption
perlima (*num*) one-fifth
permintaan (*n*) request
permisi (*interj*) good-bye; (*v*) excuse me
permohonan (*n*) request
permulaan (*n*) beginning
pernah (*adv*) ever
perpisahan (*n*) separation
persaudaraan (*n*) brotherhood
pertama (*num*) first
pertandingan (*n*) game
pertengkaran (*n*) quarrel, fight
pertiga (*num*) one-third
pertolongan (*n*) help, aid
pertukaran (*n*) exchange
pertunangan (*n*) engagement
pertunjukan (*n*) show
perubahan (*n*) change
perumahan (*n*) housing
perunggu (*n*) bronze
perut (*n*) stomach
perut isi (*adj/n*) full stomach
perut kosong (*adj/n*) empty stomach
pesan (*v*) (**memesan**) to order
pesanan (*n*) order, message
peta (*n*) map
petang (*n*) evening
petani (*n*) farmer
pil (*n*) pill
pilot (*n*) pilot
pindah (*v*) (**berpindah**) to move
ping pong (*n*) table tennis
pinjam (*v*) (**meminjam**) to borrow, (**meminjamkan**)
    to loan
pintar (*adj*) smart, clever, intelligent
pintu (*n*) door, gate
pintu masuk (*n*) entrance

pipa (*n*) pipe
pipi (*n*) cheek
pirang (*adj*) blonde
piring (*n*) plate, dish
piring kecil (*n*) saucer
pisah (*v*) to separate
pisang (*n*) banana
pisau (*n*) knife
pita (*n*) ribbon
piyama (*n*) pajamas
pohon (*n*) tree
pojok (*n*) corner
pokok (*adj*) main
pokoknya (*adj/n*) the main thing
pola (*n*) pattern
polisi (*n*) police officer
polos (*adj*) plain, simple
polusi (*n*) pollution
pom bensin (*n*) gas station
pondok (*n*) hut
popok (*n*) diaper
populasi (*n*) population
populer (*adj*) popular
porsi (*n*) portion
pos (*n*) mail, post
potong (*n*) piece; (*v*) (**memotong**) to cut, to chop
potongan (*n*) discount, style (*of clothes*)
prajurit (*n*) soldier
praktek (*n*) practice
praktis (*adj*) practical
pria (*n*) male, man
pribadi (*adj*) personal
pribumi (*n*) native
problem (*n*) (**problema**) problem
puas (*adj*) satisfied
pucat (*adj*) pale
pulang (*v*) to go home, to return, to come home
pulau (*n*) island
punggung (*n*) back

puntung rokok (*n*) cigarette butt
punya (*v*) (**mempunyai**) to have, to possess
punya siapa (*pron*) whose
pusat (*n*) center
pusing (*adj*) dizzy; (*n*) headache
putar (*v*) (**memutar**) to turn
putera mahkota (*n*) prince
puteri (*n*) princess
putih (*adj*) white
putus (*adj*) broken; (*v*) to break off
putus asa (*adj*) hopeless

R

raba (*v*) (**meraba**) to touch
Rabu (*n*) Wednesday
radar (*n*) radar
radio (*n*) radio
ragu (*adj*) (**ragu-ragu**) doubtful
rahang (*n*) jaw
rahasia (*n*) secret
raja (*n*) emperor, king
rajin (*adj*) diligent, hardworking
rak (*n*) shelf
rak buku (*n*) bookcase
rakyat (*n*) people, public
ramah (*adj*) (**ramah tamah**) friendly
ramai (*adj*) busy, crowded
ramalan (*n*) forecast
ramalan bintang (*n*) horoscope
ramalan cuaca (*n*) weather forecast
rambut (*n*) hair
ranjang (*n*) bed
ransel (*n*) backpack
rapat (*n*) meeting; (*adj*) (**rapat-rapat**) tight
rapi (*adj*) neat
rasa (*v*) (**merasa**) to feel
rata (*adj*) flat, smooth

rata-rata (*adj*) average
rawa-rawa (*n*) swamp
rebung (*n*) bamboo shoots
rekan (*n*) colleague
rempah-rempah (*n*) spices
rencana (*n*) plan
renda (*n*) lace
rendah (*adj*) low
reparasi (*n*) repair; (*v*) (**mereparasi**) to repair
repot (*adj*) busy
reruntuhan (*n*) ruins
resep (*n*) recipe, prescription
resep obat (*n*) prescription
resepsionis (*n*) receptionist
resi (*n*) receipt
resleting (*n*) zipper
restoran (*n*) restaurant
retak (*adj*) broken, cracked; (*v*) to break
robek (*adj*) torn up; (*v*) (**merobek**) to tear up
roboh (*v*) to collapse
robot (*n*) robot
roda (*n*) wheel
roh (*n*) spirit
rok (*n*) skirt
rokok (*n*) cigarette; (*v*) (**merokok**) to smoke
rotan (*n*) rattan, wicker
roti (*n*) bread
roti panggang (*n*) toast
ruang (*n*) (**ruangan**) room
ruang tamu (*n*) living room
ruang tunggu (*n*) waiting room, lobby
rukun (*adj*) harmonious; (*v*) to get along
rumah (*n*) house, home
rumah duka (*n*) funeral home
rumah makan (*n*) restaurant
rumah sakit (*n*) hospital
rumah tangga (*n*) household, home life
rumit (*adj*) complicated
rumput (*n*) grass, lawn

runtuh (*v*) to collapse, to ruin
runyam (*adj*) complicated
rupa (*n*) looks
rupiah (*n*) rupiah (*Indonesian currency*)
rusak (*adj*) damaged, not running, not working; (*v*) to damage, to stop working
Rusia (*n*) Russia
rutin (*n*) routine
ruwet (*adj*) complicated

S

saat (*n*) moment, time
sabar (*adj*) patient
Sabtu (*n*) Saturday
sabuk (*n*) belt
sabuk pengaman (*n*) seatbelt
sabun (*n*) soap
sadar (*adj*) conscious; (*v*) to realize
sajak (*n*) poem, poetry
sakit (*adj*) sick, ill, hurt, painful; (*n*) ache, pain, sore
sakit gigi (*n*) toothache
sakit kepala (*n*) headache
sakit perut (*n*) stomachache
sakit tenggorokan (*n*) sore throat
saku (*n*) pocket
salju (*n*) snow
sama (*adj*) same, identical; (*prep*) with
sama dengan (*adv*) equally, same as
sama saja (*adj*) the same
sama sekali (*adv*) at all
sama-sama (*adv*) together, to share; (*interj*) you're welcome
sambil (*adv*) while
sampah (*n*) garbage
sampai (*adv*) till, until; (*v*) to arrive
sampan (*n*) boat
sampo (*n*) shampoo

sana (*prep*) (**di sana**) there, over there
sandal (*n*) sandal
santai (*adj*) relaxed; (*v*) (**bersantai**) to relax
saos (*n*) sauce, gravy
sapa (*v*) (**menyapa**) to greet
sapi (*n*) cow, beef
sapu (*n*) broom; (*v*) (**menyapu**) to sweep
saputangan (*n*) handkerchief
saran (*n*) suggestion
sarang (*n*) nest, cage
sarat (*n*) requirement, condition
sarung (*n*) sarong
sarung tangan (*n*) glove
sate (*n*) satay
saten, satin (*n*) satin
satu (*num*) one
satu juta (*num*) million
satu-satunya (*adv*) only
saudara (*n*) sibling, sister, brother, relative
sawah (*n*) rice field
sayap (*n*) wing
sayur (*n*) (**sayuran**) vegetable
sebelah (*adv*) next to; (*n*) half
sebelas (*num*) eleven
sebelum (*adv*) before
sebelum makan (*adv/n*) before meals
sebenarnya (*adv*) actually
sebentar (*n*) while
seberang (*adv*) across
sebetulnya (*adv*) actually
sedang (*adj*) medium
sedap (*adj*) delicious
sedikit (*adj*) little, few, mild
segala (*adv*) all, whole
segan (*adj*) reluctant
segar (*adj*) fresh, healthy
segen (*adj*) reluctant
segera (*adv*) soon, immediately
segi (*n*) side

segi empat (*n*) square
segi tiga (*n*) triangle
sehat (*adj*) healthy, well
sejak (*adv*) since
sejarah (*n*) history
sejuk (*adj*) cool
sejuta (*num*) million
sekali (*adv*) again, once, very
sekaligus (*adv*) at once
sekarang (*adv*) at the moment, now
sekitar (*adv*) around, about
sekolah (*n*) school
sekretaris (*n*) secretary
selalu (*adv*) always
selamat (*adj*) safe; (*n*) congratulations
Selasa (*n*) Tuesday
selat (*n*) strait
selatan (*n*) south
seleksi (*n*) selection
selendang (*n*) shawl
selera (*n*) taste
selera makan (*n*) appetite
selesai (*adj*) completed, finished, done; (*v*) to complete,
        to finish
selimut (*n*) blanket
selokan (*n*) ditch
selundup (*v*) (**menyelundup**) to smuggle
seluruh (*adv*) all, whole, entire
semak-semak (*n*) bush
semangat (*n*) spirit, energy
sembilan (*num*) nine
sembilan belas (*num*) nineteen
sembilan puluh (*num*) ninety
sembuh (*v*) to get well
sembunyi (*v*) to hide
semenjak (*adv*) since
sementara (*adv*) temporary
sempat (*adj*) available
sempit (*adj*) tight, narrow

semua (*adv*) all
senang (*v*) to like
sendiri (*adj*) self, alone
sendok (*n*) spoon
sendok teh (*n*) teaspoon
sengaja (*adv*) deliberately
seniman (*n*) artist
Senin (*n*) Monday
senjata (*n*) weapon
sepak (*v*) (**menyepak**) to kick
sepak bola (*n*) soccer
sepatu (*n*) shoe(s)
seperempat (*num*) one-fourth
sepi (*adj*) quiet
seprai (*n*) sheet
September (*n*) September
sepuluh (*num*) ten
serangan jantung (*n*) heart attack
seratus (*num*) hundred
seribu (*num*) thousand
sering (*adv*) often
sering kali (*adv*) often
sesudah (*prep*) after
sesudah makan (*adv*) after meals
setengah (*num*) one-half
seterika (*v*) to iron
setia (*adj*) faithful
setiap (*adj*) each, every
short (*n*) shorts
siang hari (*n*) noon, midday
siapa (*pron*) who
sikat gigi (*n*) toothbrush
silahkan (*adv*) please
silet (*n*) razor
sisir (*n*) comb
sobek (*adj*) torn, ripped
sore (*n*) afternoon
stan koran (*n*) newspaper stand
stasiun bis (*n*) bus station

stasiun kereta api (*n*) train station
suami (*n*) husband
suara (*n*) voice, sound, noise
suasana (*n*) situation
subuh (*n*) dawn
suci (*adj*) sacred, holy
sudah (*adv*) already
sudut (*n*) corner
suhu (*n*) temperature
suka (*adj*) fond of; (*v*) to like
sukar (*adj*) difficult
sukur (*adj*) good; (*interj*) thank god
sulit (*adj*) difficult, hard
sumpit (*n*) chopstick
sungguh (*adv*) (**sungguh-sungguh**) really
sunyi (*adj*) quiet
supaya (*adv*) in order to, so
supermarket (*n*) supermarket
supir (*n*) driver
surat (*n*) letter, paper
susah (*adj*) difficult, sad
susu (*n*) milk
sutera (*n*) silk
suvenir (*n*) souvenir
syarat (*n*) requirement, condition

T

tabah (*adj*) patient
tabir (*n*) curtain
tadi (*adv*) just now, ago, last
tahan (*adj*) durable
tahu (*v*) to know
tahun (*n*) year
tahun kabisat (*n*) leap year
takut (*adj*) afraid, scared, frightened
tali (*n*) rope, thread
taman (*n*) garden, park

tambah (*v*) to add
tamu (*n*) guest
tanda (*n*) sign, signal, mark
tanda tangan (*n*) signature; (*v*) to sign
tanda terima (*n*) receipt
tangan (*n*) hand
tangan baju (*n*) sleeve
tanggal (*n*) date
tanggal lahir (*n*) date of birth
tanpa (*adv*) without
tante (*n*) aunt
tapi (*conj*) but
taplak meja (*n*) tablecloth
tarian (*n*) dance
taruh (*v*) (**menaruh**) to put
taruhan (*v*) (**bertaruhan**) to bet
tas (*n*) bag, purse
tas tangan (*n*) handbag
tata cara (*n*) manners
tawar (*v*) (**menawar**) to bargain, to offer
tawaran (*n*) offer, bargain
tebal (*adj*) thick
tebing (*n*) cliff
teduh (*adj*) shady
teh (*n*) tea
teka teki (*n*) mystery, puzzle
tekan (*v*) (**menekan**) to push, to press
tekanan (*n*) pressure
tekanan darah (*n*) blood pressure
teka-teki silang (*n*) crossword, puzzle
teknisi (*n*) technician
telah (*adv*) already
telapak kaki (*n*) foot
telat (*adj*) late
telegram (*n*) telegram
telepon (*n*) telephone; (*v*) (**menelepon**) to telephone
televisi (*n*) television
telinga (*n*) ear
telor (*n*) egg

telunjuk (*n*) index finger
telur (*n*) egg
teman (*n*) friend
teman kerja (*n*) colleague
tembakau (*n*) tobacco
tembok (*n*) wall
tempat (*n*) place
tempat tidur (*n*) bed
tempat tinggal (*n*) residence
tenaga (*n*) energy, strength
tenang (*adj*) calm, quiet
tenda (*n*) tent
tengah (*n*) (**tengah-tengah**) middle
tengah hari (*n*) midday, noon
tengah malam (*n*) midnight
tenggorokan (*n*) throat
tennis (*n*) tennis
tentang (*adv*) about
tentara (*n*) soldier, troop
tenteram (*adj*) peaceful
tentu (*adv*) surely, of course
tepat (*adj*) on time, precise, punctual
tepung (*n*) flour
terang (*adj*) bright, clear, light
teras (*n*) balcony
terbang (*v*) to fly
terbit (*v*) to rise, to appear
terima (*v*) (**menerima**) to receive, to accept
terima kasih (*interj*) thank you
terjal (*adj*) steep
terjemah (*v*) (**menerjemahkan**) to translate
terjemahan (*n*) translation
terkenal (*adj*) famous, well-known
terlalu (*adv*) too
terlambat (*adj*) late
terlantar (*v*) to abandon, to neglect
terlibat (*v*) to get involved
terluka (*v*) to be injured
terlupakan (*v*) to be forgotten

terminal bis (*n*) bus terminal
termometer (*n*) thermometer
ternama (*adj*) famous, well-known
terong (*n*) eggplant
tertawa (*v*) to laugh
tertib (*adj*) in order
tertidur (*v*) to fall asleep
terus (*adv*) straight
terus terang (*adj*) outspoken
terusan (*n*) canal
test (*v*) to test, to try
tetapi (*conj*) but
tiap (*adv*) (**tiap-tiap**) each, every
tiba (*v*) to arrive
tiba-tiba (*adv*) suddenly
tidak (*adv*) no
tidak keberatan (*adv*) don't mind
tidak pantas (*adj*) improper
tidak pernah (*adv*) never
tidur (*v*) to sleep
tiga (*num*) three; **tiga kali** three times
tiga belas (*num*) thirteen
tiga puluh (*num*) thirty
tikungan (*n*) intersection, corner
timah (*n*) tin
timbang (*v*) (**menimbang**) to weigh
timbangan (*n*) weight, scale
timbul (*v*) to appear
timbun (*v*) (**bertimbun**) to pile up
timun (*n*) cucumber
timur (*n*) east
tindak (*v*) (**bertindak**) to take action
tindakan (*n*) action
tinggal (*adv*) left behind; (*v*) to stay, to live
tinggi (*adj*) tall, high
tingkah laku (*n*) conduct
tingkat (*n*) storey
tinju (*n*) boxing
tinta (*n*) ink

tip (*n*) tip
tipe (*n*) type
toko (*n*) store
tolol (*adj*) idiotic, foolish, stupid
tolong (*adv*) please; (*v*) (**menolong**) to help
tomat (*n*) tomato
tombak (*n*) spear
tongkat (*n*) cane
took obat (*n*) drugstore
topan (*n*) tornado
topi (*n*) hat, cap
travel biro (*n*) travel agency
tua (*adj*) old, dark
tuan (*n*) sir, Mr.
tuang (*v*) (**menuang**) to pour
tubuh (*n*) body
tuduh (*v*) (**menuduh**) to accuse
tuduhan (*n*) accusation
tugas (*n*) duty
tugu (*n*) statue
tujuh (*num*) seven
tujuh belas (*num*) seventeen
tujuh puluh (*num*) seventy
tukang gunting rambut (*n*) barber
tukang jahit (*n*) tailor
tukang masak (*n*) cook, chef
tukar (*v*) (**menukar**) to exchange
tulen (*adj*) original, genuine
tulisan (*n*) writing
tulus (*adj*) sincere, honest
tumbuh (*v*) to grow
tumit (*n*) heel
tumpah (*v*) to spill
tumpuk (*v*) (**bertumpuk, menumpuk**) to pile up
tumpul (*adj*) blunt
tunangan (*n*) fiancé, fiancée
tunjuk (*v*) (**menunjuk**) to point, to appoint
tupai (*n*) squirrel
turis (*n*) tourist

turun (*adv*) down, go down
turut (*v*) (**menurut**) to obey
tusuk gigi (*n*) toothpick
tutup (*v*) (**menutup**) to close, to shut

U

uang (*n*) money
uang kembalian (*n*) change
uang kontan (*n*) cash
uang saku (*n*) pocket money
uang tip (*n*) tip
uap (*n*) steam, vapor; (*v*) (**menguap**) to evaporate
ubah (*v*) (**berubah, mengubah**) to change
uban (*n*) gray hair
ubin (*n*) floor
ucap (*v*) (**mengucapkan**) to pronounce, to say
ucapan (*n*) pronunciation
udang (*n*) shrimp
udara (*n*) air, climate, atmosphere
ujung (*n*) end, tip
ukir (*v*) (**mengukir**) to engrave, to carve
ukiran (*n*) carving, engraving
ukur (*v*) (**mengukur**) to measure
ukuran (*n*) measurement, size
ulang (*v*) (**mengulang**) to repeat
umum (*n*) public
umumkan (*v*) (**mengumumkan**) to announce
umur (*n*) age
undang (*v*) (**mengundang**) to invite
undangan (*n*) invitation
undang-undang (*n*) law
undian (*n*) lottery
undur (*v*) to delay
undur diri (*v*) (**mengundurkan diri**) to resign
ungu (*adj*) purple
untuk (*prep*) for

untung (*adj*) to be lucky; (*n*) profit, luck; (*v*) (**beruntung**) to profit

untunglah (*adv*) fortunately, luckily

upah (*n*) wages, earnings, benefit

upaya (*n*) effort

urusan (*n*) affair, business

usaha (*n*) effort, business

usahawan (*n*) businessman

usang (*adj*) old

usil (*adj*) curious

usulan (*n*) suggestion

utang (*n*) debt, (*v*) (**berutang**) to owe

utusan (*n*) convoy

V

vakansi (*n*) vacation

variasi (*n*) variation

violet (*adj*) violet

virus (*n*) virus

visa (*n*) visa

vital (*adj*) vital

vitamin (*n*) vitamin

W

wabah (*n*) plague

wajah (*n*) face

wajan (*n*) frying pan

wajib (*n*) obligation; (*v*) to comply

wakil (*n*) representative, deputy

waktu (*n*) time

wali (*n*) guardian, on behalf

walikota (*n*) mayor

wangi (*adj*) sweet smelling

wangi-wangian (*n*) potpourri

wanita (*n*) woman, lady

warga negara (*n*) citizen
warna (*n*) color
warna kulit (*adj*) beige
warna-warni (*adj*) colorful
warta berita (*n*) news
wartawan (*n*) journalist (*male*)
wartawati (*n*) journalist (*female*)
warung (*n*) shop, canteen, café
wasit (*n*) referee
waspada (*adj*) cautious, alert
waswas (*adj*) worried
weker (*n*) alarm clock
wilayah (*n*) area, district
wiski (*n*) whiskey
wortel (*n*) carrot
wujud (*n*) shape

Y

ya (*adv*) yes
yakin (*adj*) certain, convinced
yang lain (*adv*) another
yang lalu (*adv*) ago
yang mana (*adv*) which one
yayasan (*n*) institute, foundation
yoga (*n*) yoga
yogurt (*n*) yogurt

Z

zaman (*n*) age, era, period, time
zamrud (*n*) emerald
zat (*n*) essence, substance
ziarah (*n*) pilgrim

ENGLISH–INDONESIAN DICTIONARY

A

abandon (*v*) terlantar, menelantarkan
abbey (*n*) biara
abbreviate (*v*) memendekkan, menyingkat
abbreviation (*n*) singkatan, kependekan
abduct (*v*) menculik
abduction (*n*) penculikan
abductor (*n*) penculik
ability (*n*) kecakapan, kemampuan
able (*adj*) bisa, dapat
abolish (*v*) menghapus
abolishment (*n*) penghapusan
about (*adv*) tentang
above (*prep*) atas, di atas
abroad (*adv*) luar negeri
absence (*n*) absent
absolute (*n*) absolut
abundant (*adj*) berlimpah-limpah
abuse (*v*) menyalahgunakan
academic (*adj*) akademis
academy (*n*) akademi
accent (*n*) aksen
accept (*v*) menerima
accident (*n*) kecelakaan
accidentally (*adv*) secara kebetulan
accommodation (*n*) akomodasi
accompany (*v*) menemani
accomplish (*v*) mencapai hasil, berhasil
according (*adv*) menurut
account (*n*) perhitungan
accountant (*n*) akuntan
accounting (*n*) akutansi

accurate (*adj*) tepat
accusation (*n*) tuduhan
accuse (*v*) menuduh
accused (*n*) tertuduh
ache (*n*) sakit
acknowledgment (*n*) penghargaan
acquaintance (*n*) kenalan
across (*adv*) di seberang
action (*n*) tindakan, perbuatan
active (*adj*) aktif
activity (*n*) aktivitas
actor (*n*) aktor
actress (*n*) artis
actually (*adv*) sebenarnya
adapt (*v*) beradaptasi
adaptation (*n*) adaptasi
add (*v*) menambah, menjumlah
addicted (*adj*) ketagihan, kecanduan
addiction (*n*) ketagihan, kecanduan
addition (*n*) penambahan
address (*n*) alamat
addressee (*n*) si alamat
adequate (*adj*) cukup
adjust (*v*) menyesuaikan (diri)
adjusted (*adj*) menyesuaikan (diri)
adjustment (*n*) penyesuaian (diri)
administration (*n*) pemerintahan, administrasi
admiration (*n*) kekaguman
admire (*v*) kagum, mengagumi
admirer (*n*) pengagum
admit (*v*) mengakui
adopt (*v*) mengangkat (anak), mengadopsi
adult (*n*) orang dewasa
advance (*adj*) maju
advantage (*n*) kelebihan
adventure (*n*) petualangan
advice (*n*) nasihat
advise (*v*) menasihatkan
affair (*n*) hal, perkara

affirm (*v*) menegaskan
affirmation (*n*) ketegasan
afloat (*adv*) terapung, mengapung
after (*prep*) sesudah
afternoon (*n*) sore, siang hari
afterwards (*adv*) kemudian
again (*adv*) sekali, lagi
against (*adv*) lawan
age (*n*) umur
agenda (*n*) agenda
agent (*n*) agent, biro
agile (*adj*) gesit
aggression (*n*) agresi
aggressive (*adj*) agresif
ago (*adv*) yang lalu
agony (*n*) penderitaan, kesakitan
agree (*v*) setuju, menyetujui
agreement (*n*) persetujuan
aid (*n*) pertolongan
air (*n*) udara
air conditioning (*n*) a.c.
aircraft (*n*) pesawat udara
airport (*n*) pelabuhan udara, airport
alarm clock (*n*) weker
alcohol (*n*) alkohol
alike (*adj*) sama, serupa
alive (*adj*) hidup
all (*adv*) semua
allergy (*n*) alergi
allow (*v*) boleh
allowance (*n*) uang saku
ally (*n*) sekutu
aloud (*adv*) keras
alphabet (*n*) alfabet
altogether (*adv*) semua
amazed (*adj*) kagum
amazement (*n*) kekaguman
ambassador (*n*) duta besar
ambition (*n*) ambisi

ambitious (*adj*) berambisi
America (*n*) Amerika
American (*n*) orang Amerika
among (*prep*) di antara
amulet (*n*) mantera, jimat
ancestor (*n*) nenek moyang, leluhur
and (*conj*) dan
angel (*n*) malaikat
angry (*adj*) marah
animal (*n*) binatang, hewan
announcement (*n*) pengumuman
answer (*n*) jawaban; (*v*) menjawab
antibiotic (*n*) antibiotik
appear (*v*) tampak, muncul
appearance (*n*) kemunculan
appetite (*n*) nafsu makan, selera makan
apple (*n*) apel
appreciate (*v*) menghargai
appreciation (*n*) penghargaan
April (*n*) April
archipelago (*n*) kepulauan
architect (*n*) arsitek
argue (*v*) berdebat
argument (*n*) perdebatan
arm (*n*) lengan
army (*n*) tentara
around (*adv*) sekeliling, sekitar
arrange (*v*) mengatur, mengurus
arrest (*n*) penangkapan; (*v*) menangkap
arrival (*n*) kedatangan
arrive (*v*) tiba, datang, sampai
arrogant (*adj*) sombong
artist (*n*) seniman
ash (*n*) abu
ashamed (*adj*) malu
ashtray (*n*) asbak
assist (*v*) tolong, bantu
assistant (*n*) asisten
assume (*v*) menyangka, mengira

assumption (*n*) sangka, perkiraan
atlas (*n*) atlas, peta
attack (*n*) penyerangan; (*v*) menyerang
attempt (*v*) mencoba
attend (*v*) menghadiri
attention (*n*) perhatian
August (*n*) Agustus
aunt (*n*) bibi, tante
Australia (*n*) Australia
Australian (*adj*) Australia; (*n*) orang Australi(a) (*person*)
authentic (*adj*) asli, aseli
author (*n*) pengarang (buku)
authority (*n*) yang berwajib
automatic (*adj*) otomatis
avocado (*n*) alpokat
avoid (*v*) menghindar
awake (*v*) bangun
award (*n*) hadiah; (*v*) menghadiahkan
away (*adj*) jauh
axe (*n*) kapak

B

baby (*n*) orok, bayi
bachelor (*n*) bujangan
back (*adj*) belakang
bad (*adj*) buruk
badminton (*n*) badminton
bag (*n*) tas, dompet
bake (*v*) memanggang
balance (*n*) neraca, timbangan
balcony (*n*) teras
bald (*adj*) botak, gundul
ballet (*n*) balet
bamboo (*n*) bambu
bamboo shoot (*n*) rebung
banana (*n*) pisang
bank (*n*) bank

bankrupt (*adj*) bangkrut
bar (*n*) bar, palang pintu
barbarous (*adj*) kejam
barber (*n*) tukang cukur
basic (*adj*) dasar
basket (*n*) keranjang
bat (*n*) (**animal**) kelelawar
bathe (*v*) mandi
bathroom (*n*) kamar mandi, kamar kecil
battle (*n*) pertempuran; (*v*) bertempur
bay (*n*) teluk
beach (*n*) pantai
bean sprouts (*n*) kecambah
bear (*n*) beruang; (*v*) melahirkan (anak)
beast (*n*) binatang buas
beautiful (*adj*) cakep, cantik (*describing a woman*), bagus
beauty (*n*) kecantikan
because (*conj*) karena, sebab
become (*v*) menjadi
bed (*n*) tempat tidur, ranjang
bedroom (*n*) kamar tidur
bee (*n*) lebah
beef (*n*) daging sapi, sapi
beehive (*n*) sarang lebah
beer (*n*) bir
before (*prep*) sebelumnya, di hadapan, depan
beg (*v*) meminta-minta
beggar (*n*) pengemis
begin (*v*) mulai
behalf (*n*) (**on behalf of**) atas nama
behead (*v*) memenggal
behind (*prep*) belakang
beige (*adj*) warna kulit
belief (*n*) kepercayaan
believe (*v*) percaya verb
belong (*adv*) punya, kepunyaan
belonging (*n*) barang-barang
below (*prep*) di bawah
belt (*n*) sabuk, ikat pinggang

bend (*v*) bengkok
beneath (*prep*) di bawah
benefit (*n*) keuntungan
benzine (*n*) gas
beside (*adv*) selain itu; (*prep*) di samping
best (*adj*) terbaik
between (*prep*) antara
beverage (*n*) minuman
beware (*adv*) hati-hati, awas
beyond (*adv*) di luar, melebihi
bible (*n*) kitab suci, alkitab
bicycle (*n*) sepeda
big (*adj*) besar
bike (*n*) sepeda
bill (*n*) rekening, bon, resi
bird (*n*) burung
birth (*n*) kelahiran
birthday (*n*) (hari) ulang tahun
bishop (*n*) uskup
bite (*v*) menggigit
bitter (*adj*) pahit
black (*adj*) hitam
black-and-white (*adj*) hitam putih
blackboard (*n*) papan tulis
blacksmith (*n*) pandai besi
blank (*adj*) kosong
blanket (*n*) selimut
bleed (*v*) berdarah
bless (*v*) memberkati
blessed (*adj*) terbekati
blood pressure (*n*) tekanan darah
blouse (*n*) blus, baju blus
blue (*adj*) biru
blunt (*adj*) tumpul
blurry (*adj*) buram
boat (*n*) perahu, kapal
body (*n*) badan, mayat
boil (*v*) merebus
bomb (*n*) bom

bond (*n*) ikatan
bone (*n*) tulang
book (*n*) buku
border (*n*) perbatasan
born (*v*) dilahirkan
both (*adv*) keduanya
bother (*v*) mengganggu
bottle (*n*) botol
bottom (*n*) bawah
bow (*n*) panah
bowl (*n*) mangkok
box (*n*) kotak
boxing (*n*) tinju
boy (*n*) anak laki-laki
boycott (*v*) memboikot
boyfriend (*n*) pacar
bra (*n*) beha
bracelet (*n*) gelang
brain (*n*) otak
brake (*n*) rem
branch (*n*) cabang
brave (*adj*) berani
bravery (*n*) keberanian
bread (*n*) roti
break (*v*) pecah, patah
breakfast (*n*) sarapan, makan pagi
breath (*n*) nafas
breathe (*v*) bernafas
bribe (*v*) menyogok
bribery (*n*) penyogokan
brick (*n*) bata, batu bata
bride (*n*) pengantin
bridegroom (*n*) pengantin laki-laki
bridge (*n*) jembatan
brief (*adj*) singkat, pendek
briefcase (*n*) koper
bright (*adj*) terang, cerdas
brilliant (*adj*) cerdas, tangkas
bring (*v*) membawa

British (*adj*) Inggris; (*n*) orang Inggris (*person*)
broken (*adj*) patah, pecah, putus
broom (*n*) sapu
brother (*n*) kakak laki-laki (*older*), adik laki-laki (*younger*)
brown (*adj*) coklat
brush (*n*) sikat, sisir
bucket (*n*) ember
Buddhist (*n*) Budha
budget (*n*) anggaran belanja
build (*v*) membangun, mendirikan
building (*n*) bangunan, gedung
bunny (*n*) anak kelinci
burden (*n*) beban; (*v*) membebani
bureau (*n*) biro, agen
bureaucracy (*n*) birokrasi
burglar (*n*) pencuri
burial (*n*) pemakaman
burn (*v*) membakar
bury (*v*) mengubur
bus (*n*) bis
bus terminal (*n*) terminal bis, stasiun bis
bush (*n*) semak-semak
business (*n*) usaha, urusan
businessman (*n*) pengusaha, usahawan
busy (*adj*) sibuk, ramai
but (*conj*) tetapi
butter (*n*) mentega, margarin
butterfly (*n*) kupu-kupu
button (*n*) kancing; (*v*) kancing, mengancingkan
buy (*v*) beli, membeli
by (*adv*) oleh, dengan

C

cab (*n*) taksi
cabbage (*n*) kol, kubis
cabinet (*n*) kabinet
cable (*n*) kabel

café (*n*) cafeteria, warung kopi
cage (*n*) kandang
cake (*n*) kue, kue-kue
calamity (*n*) malapetaka, bencana
calculate (*v*) menghitung
calculation (*n*) perhitungan
calculator (*n*) kalkulator
call (*n*) telepon (*as in you have a call*); (*v*) memanggil,
    menelpon
calm (*adj*) tenang
camel (*n*) unta
can (*n*) kaleng; (*v*) dapat
Canada (*n*) Kanada
Canadian (*adj*) Kanada; (*n*) orang Kanada (*person*)
canal (*n*) terusan
cancel (*v*) batal
cancellation (*n*) pembantalan
candle (*n*) lilin
cane (*n*) tongkat
canteen (*n*) kantin
capability (*n*) kemampuan
capacity (*n*) kapasitas
capital (*n*) ibu kota, modal
captivity (*n*) tawanan
capture (*v*) menangkap, tertangkap
card (*n*) kartu
care (*n*) perawatan; (*v*) merawat
career (*n*) karir
careful (*adj*) hati-hati
careless (*adj*) sembarangan, sembrono
carrot (*n*) wortel
carry (*v*) membawa, mengangkat
cart (*n*) kereta
carve (*v*) mengukir
carving (*n*) ukiran
case (*n*) tas
cash (*n*) kontan; (*v*) menguangkan
cashier (*n*) kasir
castle (*n*) puri
casualty (*n*) korban

cat (*n*) kucing
catalog (*n*) katalog
catastrophe (*n*) bencana, malapetaka
catch (*v*) menangkap
category (*n*) kategori
Catholic (*adj, n*) Katolik
cattle (*n*) ternak
cauliflower (*n*) kembang kol
cause (*n*) penyebab, sebab
ceiling (*n*) langit-langit
celebrate (*v*) merayakan
celebration (*n*) perayaan
cemetery (*n*) kuburan
censor (*n*) sensor
center (*n*) pusat
central (*adj*) sentral
centralization (*n*) sentralisasi
century (*n*) abad
ceremony (*n*) upacara
certain (*adj*) pasti, tertentu
certainty (*n*) kepastian, ketentuan
certificate (*n*) sertifikat, akta, surat
chain (*n*) rantai
chairman (*n*) ketua
chalk (*n*) kapur
challenge (*n*) tantangan; (*v*) menantang
chamber (*n*) kamar
chance (*n*) kesempatan
change (*n*) perubahan, uang kembali; (*v*) berubah
channel (*n*) saluran
character (*n*) sifat
charge (*n*) harga, ongkos; (*v*) mengebon, membayar nanti
charisma (*n*) karisma
charity (*n*) derma, amal
chase (*n*) pengejaran; (*v*) mengejar
cheap (*adj*) murah
check (*n*) cek, pemeriksaan; (*v*) mengecek, memeriksa
cheek (*n*) pipi
cheer (*v*) bersorak

cheerful (*adj*) gembira
cheese (*n*) keju
chest (*n*) dada
chew (*v*) mengunyah
chewing gum (*n*) permen karet
chicken (*n*) ayam, daging ayam
chief (*n*) kepala, ketua
child (*n*) anak
childish (*adj*) kekanak-kanakan
chili pepper (*n*) cabe
chin (*n*) dagu
China (*n*) Cina
Chinese(*adj*) Cina; (*n*) orang Cina (*person*)
choice (*n*) pilihan
choose (*v*) memilih
chop (*v*) memotong
Christian (*n*) Kristen
church (*n*) gereja
cigarette (*n*) rokok
circle (*n*) lingkaran; (*v*) melingkar
circumstance (*n*) keadaan, situasi
circus (*n*) sirkus
citizen (*n*) warga negara, penduduk
city (*n*) kota
civilization (*n*) peradaban
clap (*v*) bertepuk tangan
clarify (*v*) menjelaskan
clarity (*n*) kejelasan
class (*n*) kelas, ruang kelas
classic (*adj*) klasik
claw (*n*) cakar; (*v*) mencakar
clean (*adj*) bersih; (*v*) membersihkan
clear (*adj*) bening, jelas
climax (*n*) klimaks
climb (*v*) memanjat
clinic (*n*) klinik
clock (*n*) jam, jam dinding
close (*v*) menutup
cloth (*n*) kain

clothes (*n*) baju, pakaian
cloud (*n*) awan
cloudy (*adj*) mendung
clown (*n*) badut
coarse (*adj*) kasar
coast (*n*) pantai
coat (*n*) mantel, baju dingin
cock (*n*) ayam jantan
coconut (*n*) kelapa
code (*n*) kode, tanda
cold (*adj*) dingin
collapse (*v*) ambruk
collar (*n*) kerah
colleague (*n*) rekan kerja, teman sejawat
collect (*v*) mengumpulkan
collection (*n*) kumpulan, koleksi
cologne (*n*) kolonye
color (*n*) warna
column (*n*) kolom, tiang
comb (*n*) sisir
combination (*n*) kombinasi
come (*v*) datang
come home (*v*) pulang
comedian (*n*) pelawak
comedy (*n*) komedi
comment (*n*) komentar
commerce (*n*) perdagangan
commission (*n*) komisi
commit (*v*) melakukan
common (*adj*) biasa
communication (*n*) komunikasi
community (*n*) lingkungan, masyarakat
company (*n*) perusahaan
compare (*v*) membandingkan
compete (*v*) bertanding, bersaing
complain (*v*) mengeluh
complaint (*n*) keluhan
complex (*adj*) kompleks, ruwet, runyan; (*n*) kompleks
complicated (*adj*) rumit, ruwet, runyam

compliment (*n*) pujian
compose (*v*) mengarang, menulis
composition (*n*) karangan, tulisan
compromise (*n*) kompromi; (*v*) berkompromi
computer (*n*) computer
concerned (*adj*) prihatin
concerning (*adv*) tentang
concert (*n*) konser, pertunjukan
conclusion (*n*) kesimpulan
condition (*n*) kondisi, syarat
conditioner (*n*) conditioner
conduct (*n*) tingkah laku, perbuatan
confess (*v*) mengaku
conflict (*n*) konflik
confused (*adj*) bingung, membingungkan
confusion (*n*) kebingungan
conquer (*v*) menaklukkan
conqueror (*n*) penakluk
conscious (*adj*) sadar
consider (*v*) mempertimbangkan
consideration (*n*) pertimbangan
consist (*v*) (**consist of**) terdiri atas
constant (*adj*) konstan
consulate (*n*) konsulat
consult (*v*) berkonsultasi
consultant (*n*) konsultan, penasihat
consultation (*n*) konsultasi
contact (*v*) kontak, berhubungan
contain (*v*) berisi, mengandung
continue (*v*) meneruskan, melanjutkan
contract (*n*) kontrak
contradiction (*n*) kontradiksi
contrary (*prep*) (**on the contrary**) sebaliknya
contrast (*n*) kontras
contribution (*n*) sumbangan
control (*v*) mengontrol
controversial (*adj*) kontroversial
cook (*n*) tukang masak; (*v*) masak, memasak
cooking (*n*) masakan

cool (*adj*) sejuk, dingin
copy (*n*) salinan; (*v*) menyalin
corn (*n*) jagung
corner (*n*) pojok, tikungan
correction (*n*) koreksi
cost (*n, v*) harga
cotton (*n*) katun, kapas
cough (*n, v*) batuk
count (*v*) menghitung, berhitung
country (*n*) negara
couple (*n*) sepasang, pasangan
courage (*n*) keberanian
cow (*n*) sapi
coward (*n*) pengecut
crab (*n*) kepiting
crazy (*adj*) gila, edan
credit (*n*) kredit
cry (*v*) menangis
cucumber (*n*) timun, ketimun
cunning (*adj*) cerdik, pandai
cup (*n*) cangkir
cure (*v*) sembuh, menyembuhkan
curious (*adj*) ingin tahu
currency (*n*) mata uang
current (*adj*) akhir-akhir ini, baru-baru ini
curtain (*n*) gorden
custom (*n*) adat
cut (*v*) memotong

D

daily (*adj*) tiap hari
dam (*n*) bendungan
damage (*n*) kerusakan
dance (*n*) tarian; (*v*) menari
danger (*n*) bahaya
dangerous (*adj*) bahaya, membahayakan
dare (*v*) berani

dark (*adj*) gelap, tua
date (*n*) tanggal, janji
daughter (*n*) anak perempuan
dawn (*n*) fajar, subuh
day (*n*) hari
daytime (*adv*) siang hari
dead (*adj*) meninggal
deaf (*adj*) tuli
death (*n*) kematian
deceive (*v*) menipu, membohongi
December (*n*) Desember
decide (*v*) memutuskan
decision (*n*) keputusan
decorate (*v*) menghias
decoration (*n*) hiasan
deed (*n*) perbuatan
deep (*adj*) dalam
deer (*n*) rusa
defend (*v*) membela
defense (*n*) pembela, pembelaan
degree (*n*) titel, derajat
delay (*v*) menunda
delegation (*n*) delegasi, utusan
deliberately (*adv*) dengan sengaja
deliver (*v*) mengantar, membawa
dentist (*n*) dokter gigi
deodorant (*n*) deodoran
depart (*v*) berangkat
departure (*n*) keberangkatan
depend on (*v*) tergantung
describe (*v*) menjelaskan
designation (*n*) tujuan
desk (*n*) bangku
develop (*v*) mengembangkan
development (*n*) perkembangan
dew (*n*) embun
diagnosis (*n*) diaknosis
dialogue (*n*) dialog
diamond (*n*) permata

dictionary (*n*) kamus
die (*v*) mati
diet (*n*) diet
difference (*n*) perbedaan, bedanya
different (*adj*) berbeda
difficult (*adj*) sukar
difficulty (*n*) kesukaran
dig (*v*) menggali
diplomat (*n*) diplomat
direct (*adj*) langsung
direction (*n*) arah, petunjuk
dirty (*adj*) kotor
discuss (*v*) berdiskusi, mendiskusikan
discussion (*n*) diskusi
disease (*n*) penyakit
dish (*n*) piring, makanan
dishonest (*adj*) culas, tidak jujur
distance (*n*) jarak
district (*n*) daerah
disturb (*v*) menganggu
disturbance (*n*) gangguan
divide (*v*) membagi
division (*n*) bagian, pembagian
divorce (*n*) perceraian; (*v*) menceraikan
dizzy (*adj*) pusing, pening
do (*v*) berbuat, membuat
doctor (*n*) dokter
doctrine (*n*) doktrin
document (*n*) dokumen
dog (*n*) anjing
doll (*n*) anak-anakan
dollar (*n*) dolar
domestic (*adj*) dalam negeri
donate (*v*) menyumbang, menderma
donation (*n*) sumbangan, derma
donkey (*n*) keledai
door (*n*) pintu
double (*adj*) dobel; (*v*) mendobelkan, melipatgandakan
doubt (*n*) ragu-ragu, keraguan

down (*adv*) turun, bawah
downtown (*n*) pusat kota
dozen (*n*) lusin
dragon (*n*) naga
draw (*v*) menggambar
drawer (*n*) laci
dreadful (*adj*) mengerikan
dream (*n*) impian, cita-cita; (*v*) bermimpi
dress (*n*) baju, baju terusan
drink (*n*) minuman; (*v*) minum
drive (*v*) mengendarai, menyetir
driver (*n*) supir
drop (*v*) menurun, menurunkan
drug (*n*) obat, obat bius
drugstore (*n*) apotek, toko obat
drunk (*adj*) mabuk
dry (*adj*) kering; (*v*) mengeringkan
duck (*n*) itik, bebek
dull (*adj*) tumpul
duplicate (*v*) menyalin
during (*prep*) selama
dust (*n*) debu, abu, tanah
Dutch (*adj*) Belanda; (*n*) orang Belanda (*person*)
dutiful (*adj*) patuh, menurut
duty (*n*) tugas
dye (*n*) warna; (*v*) mewarnai

E

each (*adj*) tiap-tiap, setiap
eager (*adj*) sangat ingin, ingin sekali
ear (*n*) kuping, telinga
early (*adj*) awal, cepat; (*adv*) pagi-pagi, kepagian
earn (*v*) mendapat, memperoleh
earnings (*n*) gaji
earring (*n*) anting-anting
earth (*n*) bumi, tanah
earthquake (*n*) gempa bumi

east (*n*) timur
Easter (*n*) Paskah
eastern (*adj*) timur
easy (*adj*) gampang, mudah
eat (*v*) makan
echo (*n*) gema; (*v*) bergema
economic (*adj*) ekonomis
economy (*n*) ekonomi
edge (*n*) pinggir, tepi
edition (*n*) edisi, terbitan
educate (*v*) mendidik
educated (*adj*) terpelajar
education (*n*) pendidikan
eel (*n*) belut
effort (*n*) usaha
egg (*n*) telor, telur
eggplant (*n*) terong
eight (*num*) delapan
eighteen (*num*) delapan belas
eighty (*num*) delapan puluh
elbow (*n*) sikut
eldest (*adj*) sulung (*describing a child*), tertua, paling tua
electricity (*n*) listrik
eleven (*num*) sebelas
embassy (*n*) kedutaan
emotion (*n*) emosi
emperor (*n*) kaisar, raja
empire (*n*) kerajaan
empty (*adj*) kosong
end (*n*) ujung, akhir
enemy (*n*) musuh
energy (*n*) tenaga, enerji
engaged (*adj*) bertunangan
engagement (*n*) pertunangan
engine (*n*) mesin, motor
engineer (*n*) insinyur
England (*n*) Inggris
English (*adj*) Inggris; (*n*) bahasa Inggris (*language*),
    orang Inggris (*person*)

enjoy (*v*) suka, senang
enough (*adj*) cukup
enter (*v*) masuk
entire (*adj*) seluruh, segala
entrance (*n*) masuk, pintu masuk
entry (*n*) masuk
envelope (*n*) amplop
envious (*adj*) iri
environment (*n*) lingkungan
epic (*n*) epik
episode (*n*) kisah
equal (*adj*) sama, sama dengan, sejajar
era (*n*) era, zaman
erase (*v*) menghapus
eraser (*n*) penghapus
error (*n*) kesalahan
escape (*n*) jalan keluar; (*v*) meloloskan diri
essential (*adj*) penting, pokok
Europe (*n*) Eropa
European (*adj*) Eropa; (*n*) orang Eropa (*person*)
evaluation (*n*) evaluasi
even (*adj*) rata; (*adv*) malah, pun
even though (*adv*) walaupun
evening (*n*) malam
event (*n*) peristiwa
eventually (*adv*) akhirnya
ever (*adv*) pernah
everybody (*pron*) semua, setiap orang
everyday (*adj*) tiap hari, sehari-hari
everyone (*pron*) tiap orang
everything (*pron*) segalanya, segala sesuatu
everywhere (*adv*) dimana-mana
evidence (*n*) bukti
exam (*n*) ujian
exchange (*v*) tukar
exchange rate (*n*) kurs
exhibit (*v*) memamerkan
exit (*n*) jalan/tempat keluar; (*v*) keluar
expense (*n*) ongkos

experience (*n*) pengalaman
expert (*n*) ahli
explanation (*n*) penjelasan
explode (*v*) meledak
express (*n*) ekspress
extravagant (*adj*) boros
eye (*n*) mata
eyebrow (*n*) alis

F

fabric (*n*) bahan, kain
face (*n*) wajah, muka; (*v*) menghadap, berhadapan
fact (*n*) fakta
factory (*n*) pabrik
factory worker (*n*) pegawai pabrik
fair (*adj*) adil
fall (*n*) musim gugur (*season*); (*v*) jatuh
false (*adj*) salah
family (*n*) keluarga
famous (*adj*) terkenal
fan (*n*) kipas angin
fans (*n*) penggemar
fantasy (*n*) fantasi
far (*adj*) jauh
fare (*n*) ongkos, biaya
farm (*n*) tanah pertanian
farmer (*n*) petani
farther (*adj*) lebih jauh
fashion (*n*) fashion
fast (*adj*) cepat
fasten (*v*) mengencangkan
fatal (*adj*) fatal
fate (*n*) nasib
father (*n*) ayah, bapak, papa
fault (*n*) kesalahan
fearful (*adj*) takut

fearless (*adj*) tidak takut
February (*n*) Februari
feed (*v*) memberi makan
feel (*v*) merasa
feeling (*n*) perasaan
female (*n*) perempuan, wanita
ferry (*n*) feri, kapal feri
fever (*n*) demam
few (*adj*) beberapa, sedikit
fiancé(e) (*n*) tunangan
fiction (*n*) fiksi
field (*n*) lapangan, bidang
fifteen (*num*) lima belas
fifty (*num*) lima puluh
fight (*n*) pertengkaran; (*v*) bertengkar
fill (*v*) mengisi
film (*n*) film
find (*v*) menemukan
fine (*adj*) bagus, baik; (*n*) denda
finger (*n*) jari tangan
finish (*v*) menyelesaikan
finished (*adj*) selesai
fire (*n*) api, kebakaran
firm (*adj*) keras, tegas
first (*num*) kesatu, pertama
fish (*n*) ikan; (*v*) memancing
fit (*adj*) cukup, pas
five (*num*) lima
fix (*v*) memperbaiki, membetulkan
flag (*n*) bendera
flight (*n*) penerbangan, pesawat (terbang)
floor (*n*) lantai, tingkat
flour (*n*) tepung, tepung terigu
flower (*n*) bunga, kembang
fly (*n*) lalat (*insect*); (*v*) terbang, naik pesawat
focus (*n*) fokus; (*v*) berfokus
fog (*n*) kabut
foggy (*adj*) berkabut

food (*n*) makanan, masakan
foolish (*adj*) bodoh
foot (*n*) telapak kaki
for (*prep*) untuk
forehead (*n*) kening
foreigner (*n*) orang asing
forget (*v*) lupa
forgetful (*adj*) pelupa
forgive (*v*) memaafkan
fork (*n*) garpu
form (*n*) bentuk; (*v*) membentuk
formal (*adj*) formal
formality (*n*) formalitas
forty (*num*) empat puluh
four (*num*) empat
fourteen (*num*) empat belas
fragrance (*n*) wangi-wangian
frame (*n*) bingkai; (*v*) membingkai
France (*n*) Perancis
free (*adj*) bebas; (*v*) membebaskan
freedom (*n*) kebebasan
French (*adj*) Perancis; (*n*) orang Perancis (*person*),
     bahasa Perancis (*language*)
frequently (*adv*) sering
fresh (*adj*) segar
Friday (*n*) Jumat
friend (*n*) teman, kawan
friendly (*adj*) ramah
frog (*n*) kodok
from (*prep*) dari
fruit (*n*) buah
frustrated (*adj*) frustasi
frustration (*n*) frustasi
fry (*v*) menggoreng
full (*adj*) penuh, kenyang
fun (*n*) senang
funeral home (*n*) rumah duka
funny (*adj*) lucu

fur (*n*) bulu
furniture (*n*) mebel
further (*adj*) lebih jauh
fussy (*adj*) cerewet, rewel
future (*n*) masa depan

G

gain (*v*) memperoleh, mendapat
game (*n*) pertandingan, permainan
garage (*n*) garasi, bengkel
garbage (*n*) sampah
garden (*n*) kebun, taman
garlic (*n*) bawang putih
gas (*n*) gas, bensin
gas station (*n*) pom bensin
gate (*n*) pintu, pintu gerbang
gather (*v*) mengumpulkan
generally (*adv*) umumnya
generation (*n*) generasi
generous (*adj*) murah hati
gentle (*adj*) lembut
geography (*n*) geografi
German (*adj*) Jerman; (*n*) orang Jerman (*person*),
       bahasa Jerman (*language*)
Germany (*n*) Jerman
get (*v*) mengambil
get up (*v*) bangun tidur
gift (*n*) hadiah, oleh-oleh
girl (*n*) anak perempuan
give (*v*) memberi
glad (*adj*) gembira, senang
glance (*n*) sepintas lalu
glass (*n*) gelas
glasses (*n*) kaca mata
gloomy (*adj*) buram
glue (*n*) lem; (*v*) mengelem
go (*v*) pergi

goal (*n*) gol, tujuan
god (*n*) Tuhan
gold (*n*) emas
good (*adj*) bagus, baik
good-bye (*interj*) mari, selamat jalan, selamat tinggal
goods (*n*) barang-barang
goose (*n*) angsa
government (*n*) pemerintah
government worker (*n*) pegawai pemerintah
grand (*adj*) besar
grandchild (*n*) cucu
granddaughter (*n*) cucu perempuan
grandfather (*n*) kakek
grandmother (*n*) nenek
grandson (*n*) cucu laki-laki
grant (*n*) dana
grape (*n*) buah anggur
grass (*n*) rumput
grateful (*adj*) berterima kasih
gravity (*n*) gravitasi
gravy (*n*) kuah, saos
gray (*adj*) abu-abu, kelabu
great (*adj*) bagus, besar
greedy (*adj*) rakus
green (*adj*) hijau
green bean (*n*) buncis
greet (*v*) menyapa, memberi salam
ground (*n*) tanah
group (*n*) grup, kelompok
grow (*v*) tumbuh, berkembang
grown up (*n*) orang dewasa
guess (*n*) terkaan; (*v*) menerka
guest (*n*) tamu
guide (*n*) pedoman
guidebook (*n*) buku pedoman
gum (*n*) (**chewing gum**) permen karet
gun (*n*) pistol, senjata
guy (*n*) orang laki-laki, pria

H

habit (*n*) kebiasaan
hair (*n*) rambut
haircut (*n*) gunting rambut
hairdresser (*n*) penata rambut
hairy (*adj*) berbulu, banyak bulu
half (*adj*) setengah; (*n*) parohan
ham (*n*) daging ham
hammer (*n*) palu
hand (*n*) tangan
handbag (*n*) tas tangan
handkerchief (*n*) sapu tangan
hang (*v*) menggantung
hanger (*n*) gantungan
happen (*v*) terjadi
happy (*adj*) bahagia
hard (*adj*) sukar, keras
hardly (*adv*) hampir, hampir tidak pernah
harvest (*n*) panen
hat (*n*) topi
hate (*v*) membenci
haughty (*adj*) sombong, angkuh
haunted (*adj*) angker
have (*v*) ada, mempunyai
hawk (*n*) burung elang
hay (*n*) jerami
he (*pron*) ia, dia
head (*n*) kepala
headache (*n*) pusing, sakit kepala
headmaster (*n*) kepala sekolah
headquarters (*n*) markas besar
health (*n*) kesehatan
healthy (*adj*) sehat
hear (*v*) mendengar
heart (*n*) jantung, hati
heart attack (*n*) serangan jantung
heat (*n*) panas; (*v*) memanaskan
heavy (*adj*) berat

heel (*n*) tumit
height (*n*) tinggi, tinggi badan
helicopter (*n*) helikopter
hello (*interj*) halo
help (*n*) pertolongan; (*v*) menolong
hen (*n*) induk ayam
her (*pron*) dia, nya
herb (*n*) jamu
here (*adv*) sini, di sini, ini
hero (*n*) pahlahwan
hesitant (*adj*) ragu-ragu
hide (*v*) bersembunyi
high (*adj*) tinggi
hijack (*v*) membajak
hijacker (*n*) pembajak
hijacking (*n*) pembajakan
Hindu (*n*) Hindu
history (*n*) sejarah
hit (*n*) pukulan; (*v*) memukul
hobby (*n*) hobi, kegemaran
hold (*v*) memegang, mengadakan
hole (*n*) lobang, lubang
holiday (*n*) hari libur, hari besar
holy (*adj*) suci
home (*n*) rumah
homemaker (*n*) ibu rumah tangga
homework (*n*) P.R. (pekerjaan rumah)
honest (*adj*) jujur adjective
honesty (*n*) kejujuran
honey (*n*) madu, sayang
honeymoon (*n*) bulan madu
honor (*n*) kehormatan
hop (*n*) lompatan; (*v*) melompat
hope (*n*) harapan; (*v*) berharap
hopeless (*adj*) tidak ada harapan, sia-sia
horse (*n*) kuda
hospital (*n*) rumah sakit
hospitality (*n*) keramah-tamahan
hot (*adj*) panas

hotel (*n*) hotel
hour (*n*) jam
hourly (*adj*) per jam
house (*n*) rumah
housekeeper (*n*) pengurus rumah tangga
how (*adv*) bagaimana
how many/much (*adv*) berapa
however (*adv*) akan tetapi, bagaimanapun
huge (*adj*) besar
human (*n*) manusia
humble (*adj*) sederhana
humid (*adj*) lembab
humor (*n*) humor
hundred (*num*) seratus
hungry (*adj*) lapar
hunt (*v*) berburu
hurricane (*n*) angin topan
hurry (*v*) bergegas-gegas
hurt (*adj*) sakit, luka
husband (*n*) suami
hysterical (*adj*) histeris

I

ice (*n*) es
ice cream (*n*) es krim
ice cube (*n*) es batu, batu es
idea (*n*) ide, gagasan
ideal (*adj*) ideal
identical (*adj*) sama, serupa
identity (*n*) identitas
if (*conj*) jika, kalau
ill (*adj*) sakit
illegal (*adj*) gelap
illness (*n*) penyakit
image (*n*) gambaran, kesan
imagination (*n*) imajinasi
imagine (*v*) membayangkan

imitate (*v*) meniru
imitation (*n*) imitasi
immediately (*adv*) segera
immigration (*n*) imigrasi
immigration office (*n*) kantor imigrasi
impatient (*adj*) tidak sabar
impolite (*adj*) kurang ajar, tidak sopan
import (*n*) impor; (*v*) impor, mengimpor
important (*adj*) penting
impossible (*adj*) tidak mungkin, mustahil
impression (*n*) kesan
improper (*adj*) tidak patut
in (*prep*) di
incident (*n*) kejadian, peristiwa
include (*v*) termasuk
income (*n*) gaji, pendapatan
incorrect (*adj*) salah, tidak benar adjective
increase (*v*) bertambah
indeed (*adv*) sungguh-sungguh, benar-benar
independent (*adj*) berdiri sendiri
individual (*n*) invidu, perorangan
Indonesia (*n*) Indonesia
Indonesian (*adj*) Indonesia; (*n*) orang Indonesia (*person*),
    bahasa Indonesia (*language*)
indoor (*adj*) dalam rumah, di dalam
industry (*n*) industri
infant (*n*) bayi, orok
infection (*n*) infeksi
influence (*n*) pengaruh
influenza (*n*) influenza, flu
inform (*v*) memberitahu, melaporkan
information (*n*) informasi, keterangan
ink (*n*) tinta
insect (*n*) serangga
inside (*prep*) di dalam
instruction (*n*) instruksi
insurance (*n*) asuransi, jaminan
intend (*v*) bermaksud, bertujuan
intention (*n*) maksud, tujuan

interested (*adj*) berminat, tertarik
interesting (*adj*) menarik
interpreter (*n*) penerjemah
interview (*n*) interview, wawancara
invitation (*n*) undangan, ajakan
invite (*v*) mengundang, mengajak
involve (*v*) terlibat, melibatkan diri
iron (*n*) besi (*metal*), baja (*metal*), seterika (*clothes*);
      (*v*) menyeterika (*clothes*)
irresponsible (*adj*) tidak bertanggung jawab
island (*n*) pulau
issue (*n*) perkara, masalah
itch (*n*) gatal
itchy (*adj*) gatal
ivory (*n*) gading

J

jacket (*n*) jaket
jackfruit (*n*) nangka
jam (*n*) selai, sele
jammed (*adj*) macet
January (*n*) Januari
jaw (*n*) rahang
jealous (*adj*) iri, cemburu
jewel (*n*) permata
jeweler (*n*) tukang emas
jewelry (*n*) perhiasan
job (*n*) pekerjaan
join (*v*) menyusul, ikut
joke (*n*) lelucon, main-main
journalist (*n*) wartawan (*male*), wartawati (*female*)
journey (*n*) perjalanan
joyful (*adj*) senang
judge (*n*) hakim
juice (*n*) air buah, air
July (*n*) Juli
jump (*v*) melompat

June (*n*) Juni
just (*adv*) baru

K

keep (*v*) menyimpan, menjaga
key (*n*) kunci
key ring (*n*) gantungan kunci
kick (*n*) tendangan; (*v*) menendang
kid (*n*) anak, anak-anak; (*v*) main-main, tidak serius
kidney (*n*) ginjal
kilo (*n*) (**kilogram**) kilogram
kilometer (*n*) kilometer
kimono (*n*) kimono
kind (*adj*) baik
kindness (*n*) kebaikan
king (*n*) raja
kiss (*n*) cium; (*v*) mencium
kitchen (*n*) dapur
kitten (*n*) anak kucing
knee (*n*) lutut, betis
kneel down (*v*) bersujud
knife (*n*) pisau
knock (*n*) ketukan; (*v*) mengetuk
know (*v*) tahu
knowledge (*n*) pengetahuan, sepengetahuan

L

labor (*n*) buruh
laboratory (*n*) laboratorium
lace (*n*) renda
lack (*n*) ketiadaan; (*v*) berkekurangan
lady (*n*) wanita
lake (*n*) danau
lamb (*n*) domba, daging domba

lame (*adj*) pincang, timpang
lamp (*n*) lampu
land (*n*) tanah, negeri
landscape (*n*) pemandangan alam
language (*n*) bahasa
large (*adj*) besar
late (*adj*) terlambat
laugh (*v*) tertawa
laundry (*n*) cucian
law (*n*) hukum, undang-undang
lawyer (*n*) pengacara, advokat
layer (*n*) lapis, lapisan
lazy (*adj*) malas
lead (*v*) memimpin
leader (*n*) pemimpin
leadership (*n*) kepemimpinan
leaf (*n*) daun
leak (*v*) bocor, membocorkan
leap year (*n*) tahun kabisat
learn (*v*) belajar
leather (*n*) kulit
leave (*v*) berangkat, meninggalkan, pergi
left (*n*) kiri
leg (*n*) kaki
legal (*adj*) resmi, sah
lend (*v*) meminjamkan
lesson (*n*) pelajaran
letter (*n*) surat
level (*n*) level
library (*n*) perpustakaan
license (*n*) surat izin noun
lie (*v*) berbohong, berbaring
life (*n*) kehidupan
light (*adj*) muda, ringan, terang; (*n*) cahaya, lampu
lighter (*n*) geretan
like (*interj*) seperti; (*n*) kesukaan; (*v*) suka
likeness (*n*) kemiripan, mirip
limit (*n*) batas
limited (*adj*) terbatas

line (*n*) garis, antrian
lip (*n*) bibir
lipstick (*n*) lipstik
list (*n*) daftar
little (*adj*) sedikit, kecil
live (*v*) tinggal, berdiam
liver (*n*) hati
lobby (*n*) ruang tunggu
lock (*n*) kunci, mengunci
lonely (*adj*) kesepian
lonesome (*adj*) kesepian
long (*adj*) panjang, lama
looks (*n*) wajah, muka
loose (*adj*) longgar
lose (*v*) hilang, kalah
lotion (*n*) lotion
love (*n*) cinta; (*v*) cinta, mencintai
lovely (*adj*) bagus, indah, cantik
luckily (*adv*) untunglah
lucky (*adj*) beruntung, mujur
lung (*n*) paru-paru

M

mad (*adj*) gila
magazine (*n*) majalah
maid (*n*) pembantu
maiden (*n*) gadis, anak gadis
mail (*n*) pos, letter
mailbox (*n*) kotak pos, kotak surat
main (*adj*) utama
maintain (*v*) merawat, memelihara
mall (*n*) mal
mango (*n*) mangga
manner (*n*) cara
manners (*n*) tata krama, tata cara
many (*adj*) banyak
March (*n*) Maret

margarine (*n*) margarin
market (*n*) pasar
marriage (*n*) perkawinan
mascara (*n*) maskara
match(es) (*n*) korek api
matter (*n*) soal, masalah
mattress (*n*) kasur
mature (*adj*) matang, dewasa
may (*v*) boleh
May (*n*) Mei (*month*)
maybe (*adv*) barangkali, mungkin
mayor (*n*) walikota
meal (*n*) makan
mean (*v*) arti
meaning (*n*) arti
measure (*v*) mengukur
measurement (*n*) ukuran
meat (*n*) daging
medicine (*n*) obat
medium (*adj*) sedang
meet (*v*) bertemu
meeting (*n*) pertemuan, rapat
member (*n*) anggota
memory (*n*) kenangan
mention (*v*) menyebutkan
middle (*n*) tengah
midnight (*n*) tengah malam
mild (*adj*) sedikit
milk (*n*) susu
mind (*n*) pikiran, otak; (*v*) berkeberatan
miracle (*n*) keajaiban
mirror (*n*) kaca
mist (*n*) kabut
mistake (*n*) kesalahan
mistaken (*adj*) salah
misunderstand (*v*) salah mengerti
mix (*v*) mencampur
mixture (*n*) campuran
Monday (*n*) Senin

money (*n*) uang
monosodium (*n*) pecin
mood (*n*) perasaan
moon (*n*) bulan
morning (*n*) pagi
Moslem (*n*) Islam
mosquito (*n*) nyamuk
mother (*n*) ibu
mountain (*n*) gunung
mouse (*n*) tikus
mouth (*n*) mulut
mud (*n*) lumpur
muddy (*adj*) becek
multiply (*v*) berlipat ganda
muscle (*n*) otot
museum (*n*) museum
mushroom (*n*) jamur
music (*n*) musik
musician (*n*) musikus
must (*v*) harus
mysterious (*adj*) misterius
mystery (*n*) misteri

N

nail (*n*) kuku, paku; (*v*) memaku
nail clipper (*n*) gunting kuku
naked (*adj*) telanjang
name (*n*) nama
narrow (*adj*) sempit, picik
nation (*n*) bangsa
native (*n*) penduduk asli, pribumi
nature (*n*) alam
nauseous (*adj*) mual
near (*adj, prep*) dekat
nearby (*adj, prep*) dekat
nearly (*adv*) hampir
neat (*adj*) rapi, apik

necessary (*adj*) perlu

neck (*n*) leher

necklace (*n*) kalung

necktie (*n*) dasi kupu-kupu

need (*n*) kebutuhan; (*v*) membutuhkan

needle (*n*) jarum

needless (*adj*) sia-sia, tidak ada gunanya

needy (*adj*) melarat, miskin

negative (*adj*) negatif

neglect (*v*) terlantar, menelantarkan

negotiate (*v*) berunding

nervous (*adj*) gugup

Netherlands (*n*) Belanda

new (*adj*) baru

newly (*adj*) baru

newspaper (*n*) koran

newspaper stand (*n*) stan koran

nice (*adj*) bagus, baik

night (*n*) malam (hari); **at night** (*adv*) pada malam hari

nightclub (*n*) klub malam

nightgown (*n*) baju tidur

nightly (*adv*) setiap malam

nightmare (*n*) mimpi buruk

nine (*num*) sembilan

nineteen (*num*) sembilan belas

ninety (*num*) sembilan puluh

no (*adv*) tidak, bukan

noble (*adj*) mulia

noisy (*adj*) bising

noon (*n*) siang hari

nose (*n*) hidung

notebook (*n*) buku catatan

notify (*v*) memberitahu, melaporkan

November (*n*) Nopember

nurse (*n*) perawat

nut (*n*) kacang

nutritious (*adj*) bergizi

nymph (*n*) bidadari

O

obedient (*adj*) patuh
obey (*v*) mematuhi
obligation (*n*) keharusan
obvious (*adj*) nyata, jelas
occupation (*n*) pendudukan, pekerjaan
occupy (*v*) menduduki
October (*n*) Oktober
offer (*n*) tawaran; (*v*) menawarkan
office (*n*) kantor
office worker (*n*) pekerja kantor
oil (*n*) oli
one (*num*) satu
onion (*n*) bawang
open (*v*) membuka
opening (*n*) pembukaan
opinion (*n*) opini, pendapat
opportunity (*n*) kesempatan
orange (*adj*) oranye (*color*); (*n*) jeruk (*fruit*)
orange juice (*n*) air jeruk
origin (*n*) asal usul
original (*adj*) orisinil, asli
other (*adj*) yang lain
owe (*v*) berhutang

P

pack (*v*) paket, mengepak
page (*n*) halaman
pain (*n*) (rasa) sakit
painful (*adj*) sakit
painting (*n*) lukisan, cat
pair (*n*) pasang
pajamas (*n*) piyama
palace (*n*) istana
pale (*adj*) pucat
panic (*v*) panik

panties (*n*) celana dalam
pants (*n*) celana panjang
papaya (*n*) pepaya
paper (*n*) kertas
park (*n*) taman, kebun; (*v*) memarkir
part (*n*) bagian
party (*n*) pesta, perayaan, partai
pass (*v*) lewat
passport (*n*) paspor
patient (*adj*) sabar; (*n*) pasien
pay (*v*) membayar
payment (*n*) pembayaran
peace (*n*) perdamaian
peaceful (*adj*) damai, tenang
peas (*n*) kacang polong
pen (*n*) pena
pencil (*n*) pensil
people (*n*) orang, rakyat
pepper (*n*) cabe, lada, merica
perfect (*adj*) sempurna
perfume (*n*) parfum, minyak wangi
permanent (*adj*) tetap
permission (*n*) izin
permit (*n*) surat izin
personality (*n*) kepribadian
persuade (*v*) membujuk
pharmacy (*n*) apotik
phone (*n*) telepon; (*v*) menelepon, telepon
pick (*v*) memetik
pick up (*v*) menjemput
pile (*n*) tumpukan; (*v*) bertumpuk, tumpuk
pill (*n*) pil
pillow (*n*) bantal
pilot (*n*) pilot
pin (*n*) peniti, bros
pink (*adj*) merah muda
place (*n*) tempat
plain (*adj*) sederhana, biasa
plate (*n*) piring

play (*v*) bermain
please (*adv*) silahkan, tolong, coba
pleased (*adj*) senang, puas
pocket (*n*) kantong
point (*n*) ujung, pendapat
police (*n*) polisi
police station (*n*) kantor polisi
polite (*adj*) sopan
pollution (*n*) polusi
pork (*n*) babi
position (*n*) kedudukan, posisi
post office (*n*) kantor pos
postcard (*n*) kartu pos
potato (*n*) kentang
pour (*v*) menuang
powder (*n*) bedak
power (*n*) kekuasaan
pregnant (*adj*) hamil, mengandung
prepare (*v*) mempersiapkan, menyiapkan
prescription (*n*) resep obat
present (*n*) hadiah
pressure (*n*) tekanan, desakan
pretty (*adj*) bagus, cantik
price (*n*) harga
pride (*n*) kebanggaan
prison (*n*) penjara
problem (*n*) problem
production (*n*) produksi
prohibit (*v*) melarang
promise (*n*) janji; (*v*) berjanji, janji, menjanjikan
proof (*n*) bukti
proper (*adj*) pantas, patut
proposal (*n*) usulan, pengajuan
propose (*v*) mengajukan, melamar
proud (*adj*) bangga
prove (*v*) membuktikan
public (*n*) umum
pumpkin (*n*) labu
punctual (*adj*) tepat

purchase (*n*) pembelian; (*v*) membeli;
purple (*adj*) ungu
purpose (*n*) tujuan
put (*v*) menaruh, meletakkan
puzzle (*n*) teka teki; (*v*) membingungkan

Q

quality (*n*) kualitas, kualitet
quantity (*n*) jumlah
quarrel (*n*) pertengkaran; (*v*) bertengkar
question (*n*) pertanyaan; (*v*) bertanya
quick (*adj*) cepat
quiet (*adj*) sepi, tenang

R

rabbit (*n*) kelinci
radio (*n*) radio
railroad (*n*) jalan kereta api, rel kereta api
rain (*n*) hujan
raise (*v*) membesarkan
rare (*adj*) jarang
rarely (*adv*) jarang
rather (*adv*) agak
raw (*adj*) mentah
razor (*n*) silet
read (*v*) membaca
reading (*n*) bacaan
ready (*adj*) siap
real (*adj*) nyata
really (*adv*) benar-benar, sungguh
rear (*adj*) belakang
reason (*n*) alasan
reasonable (*adj*) masuk akal, lumayan
receipt (*n*) tanda terima, rekening, resi
receive (*v*) menerima

receptionist (*n*) resepsionis
recognize (*v*) mengenali
recommendation (*n*) rekomendasi
red (*adj*) merah
reduce (*v*) berkurang, turun
referee (*n*) wasit
refrigerator (*n*) lemari es
refuse (*v*) menolak
registration (*n*) registrasi, pendaftaran
reliable (*adj*) bisa diandalkan
reluctant (*adj*) enggan, segan
remember (*v*) ingat
repair (*v*) reparasi, mereparasi
repeat (*v*) mengulang
report (*n*) laporan; (*v*) melaporkan
request (*n*) permohonan; (*v*) memohon
research (*n*) penyelidikan, penelitian; (*v*) menyelidiki,
    meneliti
residence (*n*) pemukiman
resist (*v*) menolak
respect (*n*) respek, rasa hormat; (*v*) menghormati
restaurant (*n*) restoran
result (*n*) hasil
retire (*v*) pensiun
return (*n*) pengembalian; (*v*) kembali, mengembalikan
reward (*n*) hadiah, imbalan
rich (*adj*) kaya
ride (*n*) naik, perjalanan; (*v*) naik
right (*adj*) benar; (*n*) kanan
ring (*n*) cincin
riot (*n*) kerusuhan, pemberontakan
rip (*v*) sobek, menyobek
rise (*v*) meningkat, naik, terbit
risk (*n*) resiko
roof (*n*) atap
room (*n*) ruangan, kamar
rope (*n*) tali
rose (*n*) bunga mawar
rough (*adj*) kasar

round (*adj*) bundar; (*n*) ronde
route (*n*) rute
rub (*v*) mengusap
rubber band (*n*) gelang karet
rude (*adj*) tidak sopan, kurang ajar
ruins (*n*) reruntuhan
rule (*n*) pemerintahan, aturan; (*v*) memerintah
ruler (*n*) mistar, penggaris
run (*v*) berlari, menjalankan (*a business, etc.*)

S

sack (*n*) karung
sad (*adj*) sedih, susah hati
safe (*adj*) selamat, aman
safety (*n*) keselamatan, keamanan
safety pin (*n*) peniti
sail (*v*) berlayar
sailor (*n*) pelaut
sale (*n*) penjualan
same (*adj*) sama, serupa
sand (*n*) pasir
sandal (*n*) sandal
satisfactory (*adj*) memuaskan
satisfied (*adj*) puas, kenyang
Saturday (*n*) Sabtu
sauce (*n*) saos
saucer (*n*) piring kecil
save (*v*) menabung, irit
savings (*n*) tabungan
say (*v*) berkata, bilang
scarf (*n*) selendang
scissors (*n*) gunting
scream (*n*) teriakan; (*v*) berteriak
search (*n*) pencarian; (*v*) mencari
secret (*n*) rahasia
secretary (*n*) sekretaris
secure (*adj*) aman

security (*n*) keamanan
see (*v*) melihat, bertemu
self (*pron*) sendiri
selfish (*adj*) egois
sell (*v*) jual, menjual
send (*v*) mengirim
sensitive (*adj*) sensitif, peka
separate (*v*) terpisah, memisahkan
September (*n*) September
serious (*adj*) serius, sungguh-sungguh
serve (*v*) menghidangkan
service (*n*) pelayanan
seven (*num*) tujuh
seventeen (*num*) tujuh belas
seventy (*num*) tujuh puluh
sew (*v*) menjahit
shake (*v*) mengocok
shake hands (*v*) berjabatan tangan
shameful (*adj*) malu
shampoo (*n*) sampo
shape (*n*) bentuk; (*v*) membentuk
sharp (*adj*) tajam
shave (*v*) bercukur
shawl (*n*) selendang
sheet (*n*) seprai
shelf (*n*) rak
shine (*v*) bersinar
shoe (*n*) sepatu
shoelace (*n*) tali sepatu
shoemaker (*n*) tukang (membuat) sepatu
shop (*n*) took; (*v*) berbelanja
short (*adj*) pendek
shortage (*n*) kekurangan
shorts (*n*) celana pendek
shoulder (*n*) bahu
show (*n*) pertunjukan, pameran; (*v*) menunjukkan
shower (*n*) hujan, mandi (pancuran); (*v*) mandi
shrimp (*n*) udang
shrink (*v*) mengerut, menyusut

shut (*v*) tutup, menutup
shy (*adj*) malu-malu, pemalu
sick (*adj*) sakit, mual
side (*n*) pihak
sight (*n*) penglihatan
sign (*n*) tanda tangan; (*v*) menandatangani
signal (*n*) sinyal, tanda
signature (*n*) tanda tangan
simple (*adj*) sederhana, mudah
sing (*v*) menyanyi
singer (*n*) penyanyi
sister (*n*) adik perempuan (*younger*), kakak perempuan
    (*older*)
sit (*v*) (**sit down**) duduk
six (*num*) enam
sixteen (*num*) enam belas
sixty (*num*) enam puluh
skin (*n*) kulit
skirt (*n*) rok
sky (*n*) langit, angkasa
sleep (*v*) tidur
sleepy (*adj*) mengantuk
sleeve (*n*) lengan, tangan (baju)
small (*adj*) kecil
smell (*n*) bau; (*v*) mencium
smile (*n*) senyuman; (*v*) tersenyum
smoke (*n*) asap; (*v*) merokok
sneeze (*v*) bersin
snow (*n*) salju
soap (*n*) sabun
soccer (*n*) sepak bola
sock (*n*) kaos kaki
soldier (*n*) tentara
something (*pron*) sesuatu
son (*n*) anak laki-laki
song (*n*) nyayian, lagu
sore (*adj*) sakit
sore throat (*n*) sakit tenggorokan
sorry (*adj*) maaf

sound (*n*) bunyi; (*v*) berbunyi
sour (*adj*) asam
space (*n*) angkasa; **outer space** angkasa luar
spaceman (*n*) antariksawan, angkasawan
spare (*n*) serep
spare time (*n*) waktu luang, waktu senggang
speak (*v*) berbicara
spell (*v*) mengeja
spelling (*n*) ejaan
spend (*v*) menghabiskan, membelanjakan
spicy (*adj*) pedas
spinach (*n*) bayam
spoon (*n*) sendok
spring (*n*) musim semi (*season*)
spy (*n*) mata-mata
squid (*n*) udang
stand (*v*) (**stand up**) berdiri
starfruit (*n*) belimbing
start (*n*) permulaan, (*v*) mulai
stay (*v*) tinggal
steal (*v*) mencuri
steel (*n*) baja
stiff (*adj*) kaku
stomach (*n*) perut
stomachache (*n*) sakit perut
stone (*n*) batu
storm (*n*) badai
straight (*adj*) lurus; (*adv*) terus
strange (*adj*) aneh
strength (*n*) kekuatan
stubborn (*adj*) keras kepala
student (*n*) mahasiswa
study (*v*) belajar
stunned (*adj*) terkejut
successful (*adj*) berhasil
suffer (*v*) menderita
sugar (*n*) gula
suit (*n*) jas
summer (*n*) musim panas

Sunday (*n*) Minggu
supermarket (*n*) supermarket
surprise (*adj*) terkejut; (*n*) kejutan
sweep (*v*) menyapu
sweetheart (*n*) jantung hati, kekasih
sympathy (*n*) simpati

T

table (*n*) meja
table tennis (*n*) ping pong
tablecloth (*n*) taplak meja
tailor (*n*) tukang jahit
take (*v*) mengambil
talent (*n*) bakat
talk (*n*) pembicaraan; (*v*) berbicara
tax (*n*) pajak
tea (*n*) teh
teach (*v*) mengajar
teacher (*n*) guru
teaching (*n*) ajaran
teaspoon (*n*) sendok teh
technician (*n*) teknisi
telephone (*n*) telepon
telephone book (*n*) buku telepon
telephone office (*n*) kantor telepon
television (*n*) televisi
tell (*v*) menceritakan, melaporkan
temperature (*n*) temperatur, suhu
ten (*num*) sepuluh
tendency (*n*) kecenderungan
tender (*adj*) lunak, lembut
tennis (*n*) tennis
thank you (*v*) terima kasih
thirsty (*adj*) haus
thirteen (*num*) tiga belas
thirty (*num*) tiga puluh

thousand (*num*) seratus
three (*num*) tiga
throat (*n*) tenggorokkan
throw (*v*) melempar
thumb (*n*) jempol
Thursday (*n*) Kamis
tie (*n*) dasi; (*v*) mengikat
tight (*adj*) sempit, pelit
tip (*n*) ujung, tip, uang tip
tired (*adj*) cape
tiring (*adj*) melelahkan
tissue (*n*) kertas tisu
title (*n*) judul
today (*adv*) hari ini
toe (*n*) jari kaki
together (*adv*) bersama-sama
tomato (*n*) tomat
tomorrow (*adv*) besok
tongue (*n*) lidah
tonight (*adv*) malam ini
tooth (*n*) gigi
toothache (*n*) sakit gigi
toothbrush (*n*) sikat gigi
toothpaste (*n*) odol, pasta gigi
toothpick (*n*) tusuk gigi
torn (*adj*) sobek
tornado (*n*) angin topan
total (*n*) jumlah, semuanya
tour (*n*) tur, perjalanan
tourist (*n*) turis
tourist office (*n*) kantor turis
towel (*n*) handuk
towel rack (*n*) gantungan handuk
tower (*n*) menara
travel (*n*) perjalanan
travel agency (*n*) travel biro
travel agent (*n*) biro perjalanan
trip (*n*) perjalanan

trouble (*n*) kesusahan; (*v*) bersusah payah
true (*adj*) benar, benar-benar
trust (*n*) kepercayaan; (*v*) percaya
t-shirt (*n*) kaos, baju kaos
Tuesday (*n*) Selasa
turn (*n*) giliran; (*v*) membelok
twelve (*num*) dua belas
twenty (*num*) dua puluh
two (*num*) dua
typhoon (*n*) angin puyuh
typist (*n*) juru ketik, tukang ketik

U

ugly (*adj*) jelek, buruk
umbrella (*n*) payung
unavailable (*adj*) tidak ada
uncertain (*adj*) tidak tentu
uncle (*n*) paman
uncomfortable (*adj*) tidak enak, risi
undecided (*adj*) belum memutuskan
understand (*v*) mengerti
understanding (*adj*) penuh pengertian; (*n*) pengertian
underwear (*n*) celana dalam
unexpected (*adj*) tidak diharapkan
unfortunately (*adv*) sayang sekali, sialnya
unhappy (*adj*) tidak bahagia
uniform (*n*) pakaian seragam
unite (*v*) mempersatukan
united (*adj*) bersatu
unpopular (*adj*) tidak populer
unreasonable (*adj*) tidak masuk akal
unsuccessful (*adj*) gagal
urgent (*adj*) sangat penting, mendesak
use (*v*) menggunakan
useful (*adj*) berguna
useless (*adj*) tidak berguna

V

vacant (*adj*) kosong, lowong
vacation (*n*) vakansi, liburan
valid (*adj*) berlaku
value (*n*) nilai
vary (*v*) bermacam-macam
vase (*n*) pot kembang
vegetable (*n*) sayur
victim (*n*) korban
victory (*n*) kemenangan
view (*n*) pandangan, pendapat, pemandangan
village (*n*) kampung, desa
vinegar (*n*) cuka
violet (*n*) violet
visit (*n*) kunjungan; (*v*) mengunjungi
voice (*n*) suara
volleyball (*n*) bola voli
voluntary (*adj*) sukarela
volunteer (*n*) sukarelawan (*male*), sukarelawati (*female*)
vulgar (*adj*) kasar, kurang ajar

W

wait (*v*) menunggu
waiter (*n*) pelayan
waiting room (*n*) ruang tunggu
waitress (*n*) pelayan
wake up (*v*) bangun
walk (*v*) berjalan kaki
wall (*n*) dinding
wallet (*n*) dompet
want (*v*) ingin, mau
war (*n*) perang; (*v*) berperang
warm (*adj*) panas
warning (*n*) peringatan
wash (*v*) mencuci

watch (*n*) (**wristwatch**) jam tangan; (*v*) mengawas
water (*n*) air, air putih
watery (*adj*) encer
wave (*n*) ombak
way (*adj*) jauh; (*n*) jalan, cara
wear (*n*) pakaian (*clothes*); (*v*) memakai
wedding (*n*) perkawinan
Wednesday (*n*) Rabu
week (*n*) minggu
weekly (*adj*) mingguan
weight (*n*) berat
wet (*adj*) basah
what (*pron*) apa
when (*pron*) kapan
where (**from**) (*pron*) dari mana
where (**is**) (*pron*) di mana
where (**to**) (*pron*) ke mana
which (*pron*) mana
whiskey (*n*) wiski
whisper (*n*) bisikan; (*v*) berbisik
white (*adj*) putih
who (*pron*) siapa
whose (*pron*) punya siapa
why (*pron*) mengapa, kenapa
wide (*adj*) lebar
wife (*n*) istri
wild (*adj*) buas, liar
will (*n*) kemauan; (*v*) akan
win (*v*) menang
wind (*n*) angin
window (*n*) jendela, loket
wine (*n*) anggur
winner (*n*) pemenang
winter (*n*) musim dingin, musim salju
wise (*adj*) bijaksana
woman (*n*) wanita, perempuan
wood (*n*) kayu
word (*n*) kata
work (*n*) pekerjaan; (*v*) bekerja

world (*n*) dunia
worry (*v*) cemas
wound (*n*) luka
wrap (*v*) membungkus
wrestling (*n*) gulat
wrinkle (*n*) kusut
write (*v*) menulis
writer (*n*) penulis, pengarang
wrong (*adj*) salah

Y

yard (*n*) halaman
yawn (*v*) menguap
year (*n*) tahun
yell (*v*) berteriak
yellow (*adj*) kuning
yes (*adv*) ya
you (*pron*) kamu, anda
young (*adj*) muda
youth (*n*) anak muda, masa muda

Z

zealous (*adj*) berapi-api
zero (*num*) nol
zipper (*n*) resleting
zone (*n*) daerah
zoo (*n*) kebun binatang

PHRASEBOOK

ETIQUETTE

Traveling in Indonesia is a pleasant experience. Knowing something of the local culture will make you feel right at home. Indonesian people are very friendly toward international visitors, and they are delighted when their courtesy is returned. Here are seven essential rules of etiquette to follow when visiting:

1. Address people with the titles *bapak* and *ibu* instead of with their first names. Use *bapak* when addressing men, and *ibu* when addressing women.
2. When making a request, always begin with the words *permisi* or *maaf*, the Indonesian equivalents of "excuse me" and "sorry."
3. After one has received a reply to one's request, always say "*terima kasih*" ("thank you").
4. Use your right hand as much as possible—it is taboo to use your left hand. Even if you are left-handed, use the left hand as little as possible.
5. Never put your arm on your waist. It is a sign of haughtiness.
6. When pointing, use your thumb instead of your index finger.
7. When leaving another's company, you should say "*mari*" or "*permisi*," the Indonesian equivalents of "good-bye."

Basic Expressions

Hello.
Halo.

Yes.
Ya.

No.
Tidak.
Bukan. (*See grammar section, page 7.*)

Please.
Silahkan.
Tolong.
Coba.

Thank you (very much).
Terima kasih (banyak).

You're welcome.
Kembali.
Sama-sama.

Excuse me.
Permisi.
Maaf.

I am sorry.
Maaf.

Good-bye.
Mari.
Permisi.
Selamat jalan. (*to those leaving*)
Selamat tinggal. (*to those staying*)

The expressions *selamat jalan* and *selamat tinggal* are formal ways of saying good-bye. They're generally used when one is going away for a while, and are roughly the equivalent of "Have a nice trip." The expression *mari* is used to say good-bye in everyday situations.

Greetings

Welcome.
Selamat datang.

Good morning.
Selamat pagi.

Good day.
Selamat siang.

Good afternoon.
Selamat sore.

Good evening.
Selamat malam.

Good night.
Selamat tidur.

Good luck.
Semoga berhasil.

Sleep well.
Selamat tidur.

Have a good appetite.
Selamat makan.

How are you?
Apa kabar?
Bagaimana kabarnya?

> Fine.
> **Baik.**
> **Baik-baik.**

How is your husband?
Bagaimana kabar suaminya?

How is your wife?
Bagaimana kabar istrinya?

Is she/he all right?
Dia baik?
Dia baik-baik?

Yes, she/he is.
Baik.

Are you all right?
Baik?

Congratulations.
Selamat.

Holiday Greetings

Happy New Year!
Selamat Tahun Baru!

Happy Birthday!
Selamat Ulang Tahun!

Merry Christmas!
Selamat Hari Natal!

Best wishes./My regards to …
Sampaikan salam buat.

Many wishes.
Banyak salam.

MEETING PEOPLE

Everyday Conversation

How are you?
Apa kabar?
Bagaimana kabarnya?

> I am fine.
> **Baik.**
> **Baik-baik.**
> **Sehat.**
> **Sehat-sehat.**

How is your mom?
Bagaimana kabar ibu?

How is your dad?
Bagaimana kabar bapak?

> She/he is fine.
> **Baik.**

I haven't seen you in a while.
Sudah lama tidak ketemu.

Where have you been?
Ke mana saja?

> I've been busy.
> **Saya sibuk.**

> I've been busy working.
> **Saya sibuk kerja.**

> I've been busy studying.
> **Saya sibuk belajar.**

Come visit us.
Nanti mampir.

No wonder.
Pantas.

Meeting New People

Upon arriving in Indonesia and meeting people there, you will find that they are less reserved than most westerners. The questions may seem more personal than you expect. Answer politely and keep in mind that they are only interested in getting to know you better. They are especially curious about life outside Indonesia.

What is your name?
Namanya siapa?

    I'm Michelle Smith.
    Saya Michelle Smith.

    My name is …
    Nama saya …

What nationality are you?
Orang apa?

Where are you from?
Dari mana?

    I am from …
    Saya dari …

    I come from …
    Saya datang dari …

| America | **Amerika** |
| Australia | **Australia** |

MEETING PEOPLE

Canada	**Kanada**
England	**Inggris**
Europe	**Eropa**
France	**Perancis**
Germany	**Jerman**
The Netherlands	**Belanda**

I'm (a/an) …
Saya …

American	**orang Amerika**
Australian	**orang Australi(a)**
British	**orang Inggris**
Canadian	**orang Kanada**
Dutch	**orang Belanda**
European	**orang Eropa**
French	**orang Perancis**
German	**orang Jerman**

Do you work here?
Kerja di sini?

How long have you worked here?
Sudah berapa lama kerja di sini?

For three months.
Sudah tiga bulan.

For a year.
Sudah satu tahun.

What do you do?
Kerja apa?

I'm a/an …
Saya …

architect	**arsitek**
artist	**seniman**

author	**pengarang buku**
barber	**tukang gunting rambut**
businessman	**usahawan, pengusaha**
cook	**tukang masak**
dentist	**dokter gigi**
diplomat	**diplomat**
doctor	**dokter**
driver	**supir**
engineer	**insinyur**
factory worker	**pegawai pabrik**
farmer	**petani**
government worker	**pegawai pemerintah**
hairdresser	**penata rambut**
journalist (*male*)	**wartawan**
journalist (*female*)	**wartawati**
judge	**hakim**
lawyer	**pengacara**
musician	**musikus**
nurse	**perawat**
office worker	**pekerja kantor**
pilot	**pilot**
sailor	**pelaut**
secretary	**sekretaris**
singer	**penyanyi**
soldier	**tentara**
student	**mahasiswa**
tailor	**tukang jahit**
teacher	**guru**
technician	**teknisi**
tourist	**turis**
typist	**juru ketik, tukang ketik**
writer	**penulis, pengarang**

Family and Marital Status

Let me introduce you to my…
Kenalkan … saya.

This is my …
Ini … saya.

aunt	**bibi, tante**
boyfriend	**pacar**
brother (older)	**kakak laki-laki**
brother (younger)	**adik laki-laki**
child	**anak**
daughter	**anak perempuan**
ex-husband	**bekas suami**
ex-wife	**bekas istri**
father	**ayah, bapak, papa**
fiancé(e)	**tunangan**
future husband	**calon suami**
future wife	**calon istri**
girlfriend	**pacar**
grandchild	**cucu**
granddaughter	**cucu perempuan**
grandfather	**kakek**
grandmother	**nenek**
grandson	**cucu laki-laki**
husband	**suami**
mother	**ibu, bu**
sister (older)	**adik perempuan**
sister (younger)	**kakak perempuan**
son	**anak laki-laki**
uncle	**paman**
wife	**istri**

Are you married?
Sudah kawin?

Yes, I am.
Sudah.

No, I'm not.
Belum.

I am engaged.
Saya sudah bertunangan.

I am divorced.
Saya sudah cerai.

How many children do you have?
Berapa anaknya?
Anaknya berapa?

> I have two children: one daughter, one son.
> **Anak saya dua: satu perempuan, satu laki-laki.**

> I don't have any children.
> **Saya belum punya anak.**

How many siblings do you have?
Berapa saudaranya?

> Five siblings.
> **Lima saudara.**

A big family.
Keluarga besar.

Are your parents still alive?
Orang tuanya masih ada?

> Yes, they are.
> **Masih.**

Is your father retired?
Ayahnya?
Bapaknya sudah pensiun?

> Yes, he is.
> **Sudah.**

> He is still working.
> **Masih kerja.**

Do you have a boyfriend/girlfriend?
Sudah punya pacar?

Yes, I do.
Sudah.

No, I don't.
Belum.

I am still single.
Saya masih sendiri. *(female)*
Saya masih bujangan. *(male)*

What is your religion?
Agamanya apa?
Agama anda apa?

I am …
Saya …

Buddhist	**Budha**
Catholic	**Katolik**
Christian	**Kristen**
Hindu	**Hindu**
Moslem	**Islam**

Getting Together

Would you join us?
Mau ikut?

Would you like to see a movie?
Mau nonton film?

Would you like to take a walk?
Mau jalan-jalan?

Could you come tomorrow evening?
Bisa mampir nanti malam?

I'll take a taxi.
Saya naik taxi.

No, I'll pick you up.
Jangan, nanti saya jemput.

> Okay.
> **Boleh.**

I'll pick you up at the hotel.
Saya jemput di hotel.

I'll take you to the hotel.
Saya antar ke hotel.

I'll take you home.
Saya antar pulang.

I'm sorry, I can't come.
Maaf, saya tidak bisa datang.

I am busy tonight.
Saya sibuk nanti malam.

I work tomorrow.
Saya kerja besok.

How about tomorrow evening?
Bagaimana kalau besok malam?

Where do we meet?
Di mana kita ketemu?

What is your phone number?
Berapa nomor teleponnya?

May I call you?
Apa saya bisa telepon?

What time do we meet?
Jam berapa kita ketemu?

> We meet at …
> **Kita ketemu di …**

Don't forget tomorrow evening.
Jangan lupa besok malam.

Aren't you going anywhere tomorrow?
Besok tidak kemana-mana?

> No, I'll stay at home.
> **Tidak, saya di rumah.**

Smoking

Do you smoke?
Anda merokok?

> I don't smoke.
> **Saya tidak merokok.**

> Yes, I smoke.
> **Ya, saya merokok.**

May I smoke?
Boleh merokok?

Do you have (a/an) …?
Ada …?

ashtray	**asbak**
cigarette(s)	**rokok**
lighter	**lighter**
match(es)	**korek api**

Miscellaneous

Where are you staying/living?
Di mana tinggalnya?

Do you live alone?
Hidup sendiri?

I rent an apartment.
Saya menyewa apartemen.

When did you arrive?
Kapan datangnya?

> A week ago.
> **Satu minggu yang lalu.**

Are you traveling alone?
Ke sininya sendiri?

> Yes, I am traveling alone.
> **Ya, sendiri.**

Is your wife coming along?
Istrinya ikut?

I am traveling with my wife.
Saya ke sini sama istri saya.

Have you been here long?
Sudah lama di sini?

> Not yet.
> **Belum.**

> Just a few days.
> **Baru beberapa hari.**

> Just a few weeks.
> **Baru beberapa minggu.**

How long will you stay here?
Mau berapa lama tinggal di sini?

> Two months.
> **Dua bulan.**

Do you like it here?
Senang di sini?

> Yes, I like it here.
> **Ya, saya senang di sini.**

LANGUAGE

Do you speak …?
Bisa …?

I speak …
Saya bisa …

I don't speak …
Saya tidak bicara …

Indonesian	**bahasa Indonesia**
English	**bahasa Inggris**
French	**bahasa Perancis**
German	**bahasa Jerman**

I speak Indonesian a little.
Saya bisa bahasa Indonesia sedikit.

You speak Indonesian well.
Sudah lancar bahasa Indonesia.

Your Indonesian is good.
Bahasa Indonesianya bagus/lancar.

Can anyone speak English?
Apa ada yang bisa bahasa Inggris?

Can you speak Indonesian?
Bisa bahasa Indonesia?

> No, I don't.
> **Saya tidak bisa.**

> A little.
> **Sedikit.**

My Indonesian is not so good.
Bahasa Indonesia saya tidak begitu bagus.

I don't understand.
Saya tidak mengerti.

I understand a little.
Saya mengerti sedikit.

I understand if you speak slowly.
Saya mengerti kalau kamu bicara pelan.

What is Indonesian for …?
Apa bahasa Indonesianya untuk …?

What does this mean in English?
Apa artinya ini dalam bahasa Inggris?

How do you spell it?
Bagaimana mengejanya?

How do you say it in Indonesian?
Bagaimana ucapannya dalam bahasa Indonesia?

What does it mean?
Apa artinya?

What does this word mean?
Apa artinya kata ini?

> It means …
> **Artinya …**

Could you please explain it?
Tolong jelaskan?

Could you please speak slowly?
Tolong bicara pelan-pelan?

Is Indonesian hard or easy?
Bahasa Indonesia susah atau mudah?

Indonesian is easy.
Bahasa Indonesia mudah.

It is not that hard.
Tidak begitu susah.

Please write it down.
Tolong ditulis.

I have a dictionary with me.
Saya ada kamus.

It is a good dictionary.
Ini kamus yang bagus.

Let me look it up in the dictionary.
Saya mau cari di kamus.

I am still learning.
Saya masih belajar.

It has no meaning.
Tidak ada artinya.

English is difficult.
Bahasa Inggris susah.

How long have you been learning?
Sudah berapa lama belajarnya?

About two weeks.
Kira-kira dua minggu.

MONEY

The Indonesian currency is the *rupiah* (Rp). The exchange rate with the American dollar fluctuates, but it is typically around Rp10,000 per dollar. Banknotes come in denominations of 1,000, 5,000, 10,000, 20,000, 50,000, and 100,000. Coins come in denominations of 50, 200, and 500. In stores it is not uncommon for one to receive sweets to compensate for change below Rp200. When exchanging money, make sure that all the Indonesian money you receive is dated later than 1997. Currency dated before then is not legal tender and can only be exchanged at Bank Indonesia offices.

Is there any bank nearby?
Apa ada bank dekat sini?

Where is the bank?
Di mana bank?

Can I change an American dollar here?
Apa saya bisa tukar dolar Amerika di sini?

How many rupiahs for one American dollar?
Berapa rupiah untuk satu dolar Amerika?

How much is the exchange rate today?
Berapa kursnya untuk hari ini?

Do you sell American dollars here?
Apa jual dolar Amerika di sini?

Do you buy American dollars here?
Apa beli dolar Amerika di sini?

Is there any commission?
Apa ada komisi?
Apa kena komisi?

How much is the commission?
Berapa komisinya?

Do you have a passport?
Apa ada paspor?

> Yes, I do.
> **Ada.**

The passport is fine.
Paspor juga boleh.

May I see your passport, please?
Boleh saya lihat paspornya?

Please sign here.
Tolong tanda tangan di sini.

Do you have a pen?
Ada pena?

Do you have an ATM here?
Apa ada ATM di sini?

Can I cash my traveler's check?
Apa saya bisa menguangkan travel check?

> Yes, you can.
> **Bisa.**

We charge two percent.
Kena potongan dua persen.

It's okay.
Tidak apa.

MONEY

Common terms:

buy	**beli, membeli**
cashier	**kasir**
commission	**komisi**
currency	**mata uang**
dollar	**dolar**
American dollar	**dolar Amerika**
one dollar	**satu dolar**
exchange	**tukar**
exchange rate	**kurs**
passport	**paspor**
receipt	**tanda terima, resi**
sell	**jual, menjual**
sign	**tanda tangan**
signature	**tanda tangan**
window	**loket**

TRAVEL

Air

I'd like to book a ticket to …
Saya mau pesan tiket ke …

How much is a ticket to …?
Berapa harga satu tiket ke …?

For how many people?
Untuk berapa orang?

When would you like to leave?
Kapan mau berangkat?

What day/date would you like?
Mau hari apa/tanggal berapa?

I'd like to leave on Sunday.
Saya mau berangkat hari Minggu.

I want to arrive there on Saturday morning.
Saya mau sampai di sana Sabtu pagi.

Do you have a flight to …?
Apa ada pesawat ke …?

> Yes, we do.
> **Ada.**

Where would you like to sit?
Mau duduk di mana?

> By the window.
> **Dekat jendela.**

How many hours is the flight to …?
Berapa jam pesawat ke …?

What time does the flight to … leave?
Jam berapa pesawat ke … berangkat?

The plane is on time.
Pesawatnya tepat.

The plane is late.
Pesawatnya terlambat.

The plane is delayed.
Pesawatnya ditunda.

I'd like to change my departure date.
Saya mau ganti tanggal keberangkatan.

Could I change the departure date?
Apa saya bisa ganti tanggal berangkat?

Do I need a passport to …?
Apa saya perlu paspor ke …?

Do I need a visa to …?
Apa saya perlu visa ke …?

> Certainly.
> **Tentu saja.**
>
> No, you don't need …
> **Tidak perlu …**

Train

Where can I buy a ticket to …?
Di mana saya bisa beli karcis ke …?

What class would you like?
Mau kelas berapa?

>Executive class.
>**Kelas eksekutif.**

>First class.
>**Kelas satu.**

>Economy class.
>**Kelas ekonomi.**

I'd like two tickets to …
Saya mau dua karcis ke …

What platform?
Peron berapa?

What platform does the train leave from?
Di peron berapa kereta berangkat?

When does the train arrive?
Kapan kereta apinya sampai?

When does the train leave?
Kapan kereta apinya berangkat?

Is it leaving on time?
Apa berangkatnya tepat?

Is it leaving late?
Apa berangkatnya terlambat?

The train has been delayed.
Kereta apinya ditunda.

Does the train have air conditioning?
Apa kereta apinya ada a.c.?

How long does the train stop at …?
Berapa lama kereta api ini berhenti di …?

The air conditioning is too cold.
Acnya terlalu dingin.

When do I arrive at Bandung?
Kapan saya sampai di Bandung?

You'll arrive at Bandung …
Sampai di Bandung …

in the morning	**pagi, besok pagi**
at noon	**siang hari**
in the afternoon	**sore hari**
at night	**malam (hari)**
tomorrow	**besok**

Local Transportation

Indonesia has a number of options for local transportation, including buses *(bis kota)*, minibuses *(opelet* or *kijang)*, and taxis *(taxi)*. Other available options include *becak* (rickshaw) and *bajaj* (a three-wheeled mini-car). When taking a *becak*, bargain before getting on.

Bus

Does this bus stop at …?
Apa bis ini stop di …?

Does this mini-bus pass by …?
Apa opelet ini lewat di …?

I'd like to get off at …
Saya mau turun di …

Could I get off at …?
Apa saya bisa turun di …?

Which bus do I take to …?
Bis apa yang ke …?

Take the bus to …
Naik bis yang ke …

Is this the bus to …?
Apa bis ini yang ke …?

How much is the fare?
Berapa ongkosnya?

Does the bus have air conditioning?
Apakah bisnya ada a.c.?

I'd like an express bus with air conditioning to …
Saya mau bis express yang ada a.c. ke …

How long does the bus stop at …?
Berapa lama bis ini stop di …?

What time does the bus leave?
Jam berapa bis berangkat?

When does it arrive at …?
Kapan sampai di …?

The bus is full.
Bisnya sudah penuh.

Taxi

Where would you like to go, sir?
Mau ke mana tuan?

Could you take me to this address?
Apa bisa ke alamat ini?

I'd like to go to this address.
Saya mau ke alamat ini.

Please get in.
Silahkan naik.

Is it far?
Apa itu jauh?

It's ten minutes from here.
Sepuluh menit dari di sini.

Please drive a little faster.
Coba jalan lebih cepat.

Please do not drive too fast.
Jangan jalan terlalu cepat.

Which house is it?
Yang mana rumahnya?

It's on the right.
Di sebelah kanan.

Here is the place.
Ini dia tempatnya.

Here is the address.
Ini dia alamatnya.

Here is the number of the house.
Ini nomor rumahnya.

Stop here.
Berhenti di sini.

Keep the change.
Ambillah kembalinya.

I'd like to rent for one day.
Saya mau sewa untuk satu hari.

How much do you charge for a whole day?
Berapa sewa satu harinya?

> A whole day is …
> **Satu harinya …**

Ferry (Ferry can either be **kapal tambang** or **feri** or **kapal feri**.)

Are there any ferries to …?
Ada kapal tambang ke …?

Does this ferry go to …?
Apa kapal tambang ini ke …?

How long does it take to get to … by ferry?
Berapa lama naik/pakai kapal tambang ke …?

How many hours to get to … by ferry?
Berapa jam naik kapal tambang ke …?

How much is the fare?
Berapa ongkosnya?

DIRECTIONS

Always begin with *"permisi"* ("excuse me") or *"maaf"* ("I'm sorry") when asking a question. Also, don't forget to say *"terima kasih"* ("thank you") after receiving an answer.

Excuse me.
Maaf.
Permisi

How do I get to …?
Naik apa ke …?

> You can walk.
> **Bisa jalan kaki.**

Is Bali Bank far from here?
Apa Bank Bali jauh dari sini?

> It's not too far.
> **Tidak begitu jauh.**

> It's five minutes from here.
> **Lima menit dari sini.**

Where does/do … go to?
Ke mana …?

Where are we?
Kita ada di mana?
Di mana kita?

Where are you going, sir?
Mau ke mana, tuan?

Excuse me, where is the …?
Permisi, di mana …?

American Consulate	**Konsulat Amerika**
American Embassy	**Kedutaan Amerika**
bank	**bank**
bus terminal	**terminal bis, stasiun bis**
church	**gereja**
drugstore	**toko obat, apotek**
garage	**bengkel**
gas station	**pom bensin**
immigration office	**kantor imigrasi**
hospital	**rumah sakit**
hotel	**hotel**
mall	**mal**
Merdeka Street	**Jalan Merdeka**
museum	**museum**
newspaper stand	**stan koran**
nightclub	**klub malam**
police station	**kantor polisi**
post office	**kantor pos**
restaurant	**restoran**
supermarket	**supermarket**
telephone office	**kantor telepon**
tourist information	**penerangan turis**
tourist office	**kantor turis**
train station	**stasiun kereta api**
travel agency	**travel biro**

It's on the left.
Di sebelah kiri.

It's on the right.
Di sebelah kanan.

Turn right.
Belok kanan.

Turn left.
Belok kiri.

Straight ahead.
Jalan terus.

Pass.
Lewat.

Stop at …
Berhenti di …
Stop di …

Where can I stop?
Di mana saya bisa stop?

Where can I park?
Di mana saya bisa parkir?

May I park here?
Apa saya boleh parkir di sini?

Is there anywhere here I can park?
Apa ada tempat parkir di sini?

Is there a parking attendant here?
Apa ada tukang parkir di sini?

How much is the parking fee?
Berapa biaya parkirnya?

Where am I?
Saya ada di mana?

I am lost.
Saya nyasar.

I am going the wrong way.
Saya salah jalan.

The traffic is busy.
Lalu lintas ramai.

The traffic is jammed.
Lalu lintas macet.

Is this … Street?
Apa ini Jala …?

Gas Station

Are there any gas stations nearby?
Ada pom bensin dekat sini?

Could you fill up my tank, please?
Tolong isi penuh tangkinya?

How many liters, sir?
Berapa liter, tuan?

How much is it per liter?
Berapa satu liternya?

> One liter is …
> **Satu liternya …**

I want ten liters, please.
Saya mau sepuluh liter.

I have a flat tire.
Ban saya kempes.

DIRECTIONS

Public Signs

Open	**Buka**
Closed	**Tutup**
Enter	**Masuk**
Exit	**Ke Luar**
Do Not Enter	**Dilarang Masuk**
No Smoking	**Dilarang Merokok**
No Trespassing	**Dilarang Lewat**
Drive Slowly	**Jalan Pelan-pelan**
Danger	**Bahaya**
Caution	**Hati-hati**
Park Here	**Parkir di Sini**
Do Not Park	**Dilarang Parkir**
North	**Utara**
South	**Selatan**
West	**Barat**
East	**Timur**

ACCOMMODATIONS

There are numerous places to stay for travelers to Indonesia. Accommodations are advertised as *hotel*, *penginapan*, *wisma*, and *losmen*.

I'd like a room please.
Saya mau satu kamar.

I'd like to stay for …
Saya mau tinggal selama …

one night	**satu malam**
two nights	**dua malam**

How much is one night?
Berapa satu malamnya?

One night is …
Satu malamnya …

For how many nights?
Untuk berapa malam?

Would you like a room with air conditioning?
Apa mau kamar yang ada a.c.?

Yes, please.
Ya, saya mau yang ada a.c.

I'd like a room with (a) …
Saya mau kamar yang ada …

balcony	**teras**
hot water	**air panas**
private bathroom	**kamar mandi sendiri**
television	**televisi**

Do you have a television set in the room?
Apa ada televisi di kamar?

The room is too cold.
Kamarnya terlalu dingin.

The room is too hot.
Kamarnya terlalu panas.

The room is too small.
Kamarnya terlalu kecil.

I want a bigger room.
Saya mau kamar yang lebih besar.

I want a smaller room.
Saya mau kamar yang lebih kecil.

Do you have a bigger room?
Ada kamar yang lebih besar?

I'm sorry, the air conditioning is not working.
Maaf, acnya rusak jalan.
Maaf, acnya tidak jalan.

The television is off.
Televisinya mati.

The light is off.
Lampunya mati.

Are there any restaurants near here?
Apa ada restoran dekat sini?

Please wake me up at …
Tolong bangunkan saya pada jam …

What time do you serve breakfast?
Jam berapa makan paginya?

Please bring the breakfast to the room.
Tolong bawa sarapannya ke kamar.

Could you sleep?
Bisa tidur?

> Yes, I slept well.
> **Ya, saya tidur nyenyak.**

It's quiet here.
Di sini tenang.
Di sini sepi.

It's noisy here.
Di sini bising.

I need another blanket.
Saya mau satu selimut lagi.

I'd like to check out.
Saya mau keluar.

Could you sign here?
Tolong tanda tangan di sini?

Common terms:

air conditioning	**a.c.**
alarm clock	**weker**
ashtray	**asbak**
balcony	**teras**
bathroom	**kamar mandi, kamar kecil**
bed	**tempat tidur**
double bed	**tempat tidur untuk dua orang**
single bed	**tempat tidur untuk satu orang**
blanket	**selimut**

clean	**bersih**
clothes hanger	**gantungan baju**
conditioner	**conditioner**
curtain	**gorden**
dirty/soiled	**kotor**
dry	**kering**
floor	**lantai**
have a bath/shower	**mandi**
iron	**seterika**
lamp, light	**lampu**
lobby	**ruang tunggu**
mattress	**kasur**
mirror	**kaca**
noisy	**bising**
pillow	**bantal**
quiet	**tenang, sepi**
receptionist	**resepsionis**
room	**kamar**
small room	**kamar yang kecil**
shampoo	**sampo**
sheet	**seprai**
sleep	**tidur**
sleep well	**tidur nyenyak**
soap	**sabun**
telephone	**telepon**
telephone book	**buku telepon**
television	**televisi**
toothpaste	**odol, pasta gigi**
towel	**handuk**
towel rack	**gantungan handuk**
wet	**basah**

FOOD & DRINK

Indonesia has a variety of restaurants and eateries. The word "restaurant" is translated as *restoran* or *rumah makan* (*lit.* home to eat). You will also find many *warung* along the streets. These are temporary set-ups, with large tents and long benches. They serve primarily local dishes, and usually only one or two types of food, such as noodles or *satay*. The *warung* are ideal if you are looking for quick, inexpensive food and an informal, comfortable place in which to eat it.

In some restaurants, there is a bowl of water at the table. This is for washing your hands both before and after the meal.

You call a male waiter *mas* unless he is middle-aged or older, in which case you would call him *bapak*. Younger waitresses are called *mbak*, and older ones should be called *ibu*.

Where is a good restaurant?
Di mana restoran yang enak?

Where is an inexpensive restaurant?
Di mana restoran yang murah?

Are there any inexpensive restaurants nearby?
Ada restoran yang murah di sini?

Ordering

It's on one bill.
Bonnya jadi satu.

It's a separate bill.
Bonnya pisah.

That is fine.
Boleh.

Do you have a menu?
Apa ada menu?
Apa ada daftar makanan?

Here is the menu.
Ini menunya.
Ini daftar makanannya.

What would you like to eat?
Mau makan apa?

Give us a few minutes, please.
Sebentar.

I'd like …
Saya mau …

I'd like to order now.
Saya mau pesan sekarang.

What would you like to order?
Mau pesan apa?

Would you like one portion?
Mau satu porsi?

I'd like one portion.
Saya mau satu porsi.

I'd like a half portion.
Saya mau setengah porsi.

The same for me.
Saya sama.

Do you want anything else?
Mau apa lagi?

That's all.
Itu saja.

Would you like it with …?
Mau pakai apa …?

I'd like it with …, please.
Saya mau pakai ….

A lot of …, please!
Banyak …, ya!

Not too much …, please.
Jangan banyak ….

No …, please.
Jangan pakai ….

chili pepper	**cabe**
garlic	**bawang putih**
meat	**daging**
onions	**bawang**
sugar	**gula**
vegetables	**sayur**

Would you like it …?
Mau …?

hot/spicy	**pedas**
a little hot	**sedikit pedas, pedas sedikit**
not too hot	**jangan terlalu pedas, jangan pedas-pedas**
very hot	**pedas sekali**
too hot	**sedikit pedas**
mild	**sedikit**
medium	**sedang**

Is this hot?
Ini pedas?
Apa ini pedas?

I want it a little hot/spicy.
Saya mau sedikit pedas.

I can't eat this.
Saya tidak bisa makan ini.

This is not hot.
Ini tidak or kurang pedas.

I want a lot of …
Saya mau banyak …

May I have some more …?
Bisa tambah …?

gravy	**kuah**
pepper	**cabe, lada, merica**
salt	**garam**
sauce	**saos**
sugar	**gula**
vinegar	**cuka**

Could we have a/an …?
Bisa minta …?

ashtray	**asbak**
extra plate	**piring satu lagi**
menu	**menu, daftar makanan**

Do you have a …?
Ada …?

bowl	**mangkok**
cup	**cangkir**
fork	**garpu**
glass	**gelas**
knife	**pisau**
plate	**piring**
large plate	**piring besar**
small plate	**piring kecil**
saucer	**piring kecil**
spoon	**sendok**
large spoon	**sendok besar**
small spoon	**sendok kecil**
teaspoon	**sendok teh**

The food is good.
Masakannya enak.

It's very delicious.
Enak sekali.

I'd like the bill, please.
Minta bonnya.

Where do we pay?
Kami bayar di mana?

How much is it altogether?
Berapa semuanya?

Keep the change.
Ambil kembalinya.

Is there a bathroom here?
Apa ada kamar kecil di sini?
Apa ada w.c. di sini?

Where is the bathroom?
Di mana kamar kecil?
Di mana w.c.?

Excuse me. I'd like to use the bathroom, please.
Permisi. Saya mau ke belakang.

Fruit

apple	**apel**
avocado	**alpokat**
banana	**pisang**
durian	**durian**
fruit	**buah**
grape	**anggur**
jackfruit	**nangka**
mango	**mangga**
mangosteen	**manggis**
orange	**jeruk**
papaya	**pepaya**
starfruit	**belimbing**

Vegetables

bamboo shoots	**rebung**
bean sprouts	**kecambah**
cabbage	**kol, kubis**
carrot	**wortel**
cauliflower	**kembang kol**
corn	**jagung**
cucumber	**ketimun, timun**
eggplant	**terong**
garlic	**bawang putih**
green bean	**buncis**
green onion	**daun bawang**
mushroom	**jamur**
onion	**bawang**

peas	kacang polong
potato	kentang
spinach	bayam
tomato	tomat
vegetable	sayur

Dairy

butter	mentega
cheese	keju
margarine	margarin
milk	susu
canned milk	susu kaleng
fresh cold milk	susu segar
powdered milk	susu bubuk

Beverages

beer	bir
juice	air
apple juice	air apel
grape juice	air anggur
orange juice	air jeruk
tomato juice	air tomat
tea	teh
bottled tea	teh botol
hot tea	teh panas
tea with sugar	teh manis
water	air, air putih
cold water	air dingin
cold water w/ice	air dingin pakai es
ice water	air es
whiskey	wiski
wine	anggur
ice	es
ice cube	es batu, batu es

Meat

beef	**sapi**
chicken	**ayam**
breast	**dada**
leg	**kaki**
thigh	**paha**
wing	**sayap**
duck	**bebek**
frog	**kodok**
lamb	**domba**
meat	**daging**
pork	**babi**

Seafood

crab	**kepiting**
eel	**belut**
fish	**ikan**
shrimp	**udang**
squid	**cumi-cumi**

Dessert

cake	**kue-kue**
ice cream	**es krim**

Miscellaneous

bill	**bon**
full	**kenyang**
monosodium	**pecin**
restaurant	**restoran**
table	**meja**
tablecloth	**taplak meja**
thirsty	**haus**
tip	**tip, uang tip**
toothpick	**tusuk gigi**

SHOPPING

Where can I buy/find …?
Di mana saya bisa beli …?

Where is the nearest market?
Di mana pasar yang paling dekat?

Are there any shops near here?
Ada toko yang dekat sini?

Do you sell … here?
Di sini ada jual …?

Do you have …?
Apa ada …?

I am just looking.
Saya cuma lihat-lihat.

I am looking for …
Saya mencari …

I'd like …
Saya mau …

I'd like to see this.
Saya mau lihat yang ini.

Can I see it/them?
Boleh saya lihat?

How many do you want?
Mau berapa banyak?

Which one do you want?
Mau yang mana?

Is there anything else?
Apa lagi?

This is expensive.
Ini mahal.

That is cheap.
Itu murah.

This one is cheaper.
Yang ini lebih murah.

That one is more expensive.
Yang itu lebih mahal.

I like this one.
Saya suka yang ini.

I like that one.
Saya suka yang itu.

I don't like it/them.
Saya tidak suka yang ini/itu.

I don't want this/that.
Saya tidak mau yang ini/itu.

I'll take this one.
Saya ambil yang ini.

I want this one.
Saya mau yang ini.

I'd like to buy …
Saya mau beli …

Where do I pay?
Di mana saya bayar?

What does it cost?
Berapa?
Berapa harganya?

How much is it altogether?
Berapa semuanya?

May I bargain?
Boleh tawar?

> Certainly.
> **Boleh saja.**
> **Tentu saja.**

Could you reduce the price?
Bisa kurang harganya?

Could you lower the price a little?
Bisa kurang sedikit harganya?

I don't have cash with me.
Saya tidak ada uang kontan.

Do you accept credit cards?
Bisa bayar pakai kartu kredit?

I don't have small change.
Saya tidak ada uang kecil.

Here is the money.
Ini uangnya.

Here is the change.
Ini kembalinya/uang kembali.

Clothes and Accessories

bag	**tas, dompet**
belt	**sabuk, ikat pinggang**
blouse	**blus, baju blus**
bra	**beha**
bracelet	**gelang**
button	**kancing**
clothes	**baju**
collar	**kerah**
dress	**baju terusan**
earring	**anting-anting**
handbag	**tas tangan**
jacket	**jaket**
lace	**renda**
necklace	**kalung**
necktie	**dasi kupu-kupu**
nightgown	**baju tidur**
pajamas	**piyama**
panties	**celana dalam**
pants	**celana panjang**
pin	**bros**
pocket	**kantong**
sandals	**sandal**
scarf, shawl	**selendang**
shirt	**kemeja**
shoes	**sepatu**
shorts	**celana pendek**
skirt	**rok**
sleeve	**lengan, tangan (baju)**
sock	**kaos kaki**
suit	**jas**
tie	**dasi**
t-shirt	**kaos, baju kaos**
underwear	**celana dalam**
wallet	**dompet**
zipper	**resleting**

Colors

What color would you like?
Mau warna apa?

I don't like this color.
Saya tidak suka warna ini.

Do you have any other colors?
Apa ada warna yang lain?

This color is too dark.
Warna ini terlalu gelap.

Do you have a light color?
Ada warna yang muda?
Ada warna yang terang?

I'd like the … one.
Saya mau yang ….

Common colors:

beige	**warna kulit**
black	**hitam**
blue	**biru**
light blue	**biru muda, biru terang**
dark blue	**biru tua, biru gelap**
brown	**coklat**
gray	**abu-abu, kelabu**
green	**hijau**
orange	**oranye**
pink	**merah muda**
purple	**ungu**
red	**merah**
violet	**violet**
white	**putih**
yellow	**kuning**

light	**muda, terang**
dark	**tua, gelap**

Size

What size do you wear?
Pakai ukuran berapa?

> I wear a small size.
> **Saya pakai ukuran kecil.**

small	**kecil**
medium	**sedang**
large	**besar**

Fitting/Tailoring

This blouse is too tight.
Blus ini terlalu sempit.

This doesn't fit.
Ini tidak cukup.
Ini tidak pas.

The sleeves are too long.
Tangannya terlalu panjang.

The collar is too wide.
Kerahnya terlalu lebar.

The pockets are deep.
Kantongnya dalam.

The pockets are shallow.
Kantongnya pendek.

The zipper is broken.
Resletingnya patah.
Resletingnya rusak.

Common terms:

fit	**cukup, pas**
loose	**longgar**
tight	**sempit**
(too) big	**(terlalu) besar**
(too) long	**(terlalu) panjang**
(too) short	**(terlalu) pendek**
(too) small	**(terlalu) kecil**
(too) wide	**(terlalu) lebar**
torn, ripped	**sobek**
wrinkle	**kusut**

Can I try them/it on?
Bisa saya coba?

Is there a mirror?
Ada kaca?

Is there a fitting room?
Ada kamar coba?

Where is the fitting room?
Di mana kamar coba?

Is this cotton?
Apa ini katun?

Is this leather?
Apa ini kulit?

Will it shrink?
Apa nanti mengkerut?

Toiletries

Do you sell … here?
Ada jual … di sini?

I'd like (a) …, please.
Saya mau ….

cologne	**kolonye**
comb	**sisir**
conditioner	**conditioner**
deodorant	**deodoran**
lipstick	**lipstik**
lotion	**lotion**
mascara	**maskara**
nail clipper	**gunting kuku**
perfume	**parfum, minyak wangi**
pin	**peniti**
powder	**bedak**
razor	**silet**
safety pin	**peniti**
shampoo	**sampo**
soap	**sabun**
tissue	**kertas tisu**
toothbrush	**sikat gigi**
toothpaste	**odol**

Stationery

Do you sell (a/an) …?
Apa ada jual …?

Common terms:

book(s)	**buku**
guidebook	**buku pedoman**
notebook	**buku catatan**
calculator	**kalkulator**

dictionary	**kamus**
English-language	**kamus bahasa Inggris**
pocket	**kamus kantong**
envelope	**amplop**
glue	**lem**
ink	**tinta**
magazine	**majalah**
English-language	**majalah bahasa Inggris**
newspaper	**koran**
English edition	**edisi bahasa Inggris**
English-language	**koran bahasa Inggris**
pen	**pena**
pencil	**pensil**
postcard	**kartu pos**
rubber band	**gelang karet**
ruler	**mistar, penggaris**
scissors	**gunting**
small	**gunting kecil**
large	**gunting besar**

Photography

Do you sell film?
Ada jual film?

Do you sell cameras?
Ada jual kamera?

I'd like a roll of film, please.
Saya mau satu rol film.

What kind of film?
Film apa?

I want …
Saya mau …

black-and-white film	**film hitam putih**
color film	**film berwarna**

Could you process this film?
Bisa cuci film ini?

I'd like to develop this film.
Saya mau cuci dan cetak film.

What size?
Ukuran berapa?

>   Four by six.
>   **Empat kali enam.**

>   Five by seven.
>   **Lima kali tujuh.**

How much does it cost to develop film?
Berapa harga cuci satu roll film?

When can I pick it up?
Kapan bisa diambilnya?

My camera is jammed.
Kamera saya macet.

The shutter is not working.
Tutup lensanya tidak jalan/macet.

It may be the battery.
Mungkin baterainya.

Can you fix it?
Bisa betulkan?
Bisa direparasi?

How much do you charge?
Berapa ongkosnya?

SPORTS

Can you play golf?
Bisa main golf?

I don't play badminton.
Saya tidak bisa badminton.

I am not interested in sports.
Saya tidak tertarik dengan sport.

Who won?
Siapa yang menang?

Which team lost?
Tim mana yang kalah?

Common terms:

against	**lawan**
badminton	**badminton**
fans	**penggemar**
football/soccer	**sepak bola**
game	**pertandingan, game**
lost	**kalah**
referee	**wasit**
table tennis	**ping pong**
tennis	**tennis**
volleyball	**bola voli**
win	**menang**
wrestling	**gulat**

HEALTH

I am not feeling well.
Saya tidak enak badan.

I have a fever.
Saya demam.

I have a headache.
Saya sakit kepala.

I have a stomachache.
Saya sakit perut.

I threw up.
Saya muntah-muntah.

I am dizzy.
Saya pusing.
Kepala saya pusing.

I am sick.
Saya merasa mual.
Saya sakit.

I am coughing.
Saya batuk-batuk.

I am catching a cold.
Saya masuk angin.

My body is aching.
Badan saya sakit-sakit.

My … hurts.
… saya sakit.

body	**badan**
head	**kepala**

leg	kaki
stomach	perut

Let me examine you.
Mari saya periksa.

Where does it hurt?
Di mana sakitnya?
Sakitnya di mana?

You must stay in the hospital.
Anda harus diopname di rumah sakit.

When will I be released?
Kapan saya keluar?
Kapan boleh pulang?

What room will I be in?
Saya di kamar berapa?

Your temperature is high.
Suhu badannya tinggi.

You need rest.
Anda perlu istirahat.

Sleep a lot.
Banyak-banyak tidur.

You'll be fine soon.
Anda cepat sembuh.

Are you well?
Sudah baik?
Sudah sembuh?

I am well.
Saya sudah baik.
Saya sudah sembuh.

HEALTH

I am feeling a little better.
Saya merasa lebih baik.
Saya merasa agak baik.

I'll give you a prescription.
Saya akan kasih resep.

Take the medicine twice a day.
Makan obatnya dua kali sehari.

Take the medicine. *(If medicine is a liquid.)*
Minum obat.

Where is the pharmacy?
Di mana apotik?

Common terms:

ache	**sakit**
allergy	**alergi**
blood pressure	**tekanan darah**
cold	**dingin**
catch a cold	**masuk angin**
cough	**batuk**
dizzy	**pusing**
fever	**demam**
headache	**pusing, sakit kepala**
heart attack	**serangan jantung**
ill	**sakit**
illness	**penyakit**
infection	**infeksi**
influenza	**influenza, flu**
itch	**gatal**
nausea	**mual**
pain	**sakit**
sick	**sakit, mual**
sore	**sakit**
sore throat	**sakit tenggorokan**
stomachache	**sakit perut**

toothache	**sakit gigi**
wound	**luka**
antibiotic	**antibiotik**
medicine	**obat**
cough medicine	**obat batuk**
pharmacy	**apotik**
pill	**pil**
sleeping pill	**obat tidur**
prescription	**resep, resep obat**
after meals	**sesudah makan**
before meals	**sebelum makan**
empty stomach	**perut kosong**
full stomach	**perut isi**
once a day	**satu kali sehari**
twice a day	**dua kali sehari**
three times a day	**tiga kali sehari**
one tablespoon	**satu sendok makan**
one teaspoon	**satu sendok teh**

Parts of the Body

arm	**lengan**
body	**badan**
cheek	**pipi**
chest	**dada**
chin	**dagu**
ear	**telinga, kuping**
eye	**mata**
eyebrow	**alis**
face	**muka**
finger	**jari**
foot	**telapak kaki**
forehead	**kening**
hair	**rambut**

hand	**tangan**
head	**kepala**
heart	**jantung**
heel	**tumit**
jaw	**rahang**
kidney	**ginjal**
knee	**betis**
leg	**kaki**
lip	**bibir**
liver	**hati**
lung	**paru-paru**
mouth	**mulut**
muscle	**otot**
neck	**leher**
nose	**hidung**
shoulder	**bahu**
skin	**kulit**
stomach	**perut**
throat	**tenggorokkan**
thumb	**jempol**
toe	**jari kaki**
tongue	**lidah**
tooth	**gigi**

NUMBERS & TIME

Cardinal Numbers

1	satu
2	dua
3	tiga
4	empat
5	lima
6	enam
7	tujuh
8	delapan
9	sembilan
10	sepuluh
11	sebelas
12	dua belas
13	tiga belas
14	empat belas
15	lima belas
16	enam belas
17	tujuh belas
18	delapan belas
19	sembilan belas
20	dua puluh
23	dua puluh tiga
30	tiga puluh
34	tiga puluh empat
40	empat puluh
45	empat puluh lima
50	lima puluh
55	lima puluh lima
60	enam puluh
66	enam puluh enam
70	tujuh puluh
77	tujuh puluh tujuh
80	delapan puluh
88	delapan puluh delapan
90	sembilan puluh

99	**sembilan puluh sembilan**
100	**seratus**
102	**seratus dua**
110	**seratus sepuluh**
118	**seratus delapan belas**
155	**seratus lima puluh lima**
200	**dua ratus**
300	**tiga ratus**
1,000	**seribu**
1,500	**seribu lima ratus**
2,000	**dua ribu**
3,000	**tiga ribu**
100,000	**seratus ribu**
1,000,000	**sejuta, satu juta**

Ordinal Numbers

1st	**kesatu, pertama**
2nd	**kedua**
3rd	**ketiga**
4th	**keempat**
5th	**kelima**
6th	**keenam**
7th	**ketujuh**
8th	**kedelapan**
9th	**kesembilan**
10th	**kesepuluh**
11th	**kesebelas**
12th	**kedua belas**
13th	**ketiga belas**
14th	**keempat belas**
15th	**kelima belas**
16th	**keenam belas**
17th	**ketujuh belas**
18th	**kedelapan belas**
19th	**kesembilan belas**
20th	**kedua puluh**
21st	**kedua puluh satu**

30th	**ketiga puluh**
32nd	**ketiga puluh dua**
40th	**keempat puluh**
43rd	**keempat puluh tiga**
50th	**kelima puluh**
54th	**kelima puluh empat**
60th	**keenam puluh**
70th	**ketujuh puluh**
80th	**kedelapan puluh**
90th	**kesembilan puluh**
100th	**keseratus**
200th	**kedua ratus**
1,000th	**keseribu**

Fractions

one-half (½)	**setengah**
one-third (⅓)	**pertiga**
two-thirds (⅔)	**dua pertiga**
one-fourth (¼)	**seperempat**
three-fourths (¾)	**tiga perempat**
one-fifth (⅕)	**satu perlima**
three-fifths (⅗)	**tiga perlima**

Months

January	**Januari**
February	**Februari**
March	**Maret**
April	**April**
May	**Mei**
June	**Juni**
July	**Juli**
August	**Agustus**
September	**September**
October	**Oktober**

| November | **Nopember** |
| December | **Desember** |

| in June | **pada bulan Juni** |
| in March | **pada bulan Maret** |

The word *bulan* (month) may appear before the name of the month. Therefore, one may hear either *Januari* or *bulan Januari*.

Date

Note that the cardinal numbers, not the ordinals, are used for dates.

What is the date today?
Tanggal berapa hari ini?

It's February 1st.
Tanggal satu Februari.

It's December 8th.
Tanggal delapan Desember.

On March 3rd …
Pada tanggal tiga Maret …

Time

What time is it?
Jam berapa sekarang?

It's one o'clock.
Jam satu.

It's two o'clock.
Jam dua.

It's five to ten.
Jam sepuluh kurang lima.

It's twenty past eleven.
Jam sebelas lebih dua puluh.
Jam sebelas lewat dua puluh.

It's a quarter past nine.
Jam sembilan lewat seperempat.
Jam sembilan lebih seperempat.

It's a quarter to six.
Jam enam kurang seperempat.

It's half past three.
Jam setengah empat.

It's two fifteen.
Jam dua lima belas.

It's four thirty.
Jam empat tiga puluh.

It's two forty-five.
Jam dua empat lima

The Indonesian equivalent of "a.m." is *pagi*, and it lasts from 1 a.m. through 11 a.m. There are different equivalents for "p.m.," depending on the time of day. Between noon and 2 p.m., it is *siang*. Between 3 and 6 p.m., it is *sore*. And from 7 p.m. through midnight, it is *malam*.

It is 5 a.m.
Jam lima pagi.

It is 10 a.m.
Jam sepuluh pagi.

It is 1 p.m.
Jam satu siang.

It is 4 p.m.
Jam empat sore.

It is 8 p.m.
Jam delapan malam.

How many hours?
Berapa jam?

> For five hours.
> **Selama lima jam.**
>
> In two hours.
> **Dua jam lagi.**
>
> Two hours ago.
> **Dua jam yang lalu.**

How many minutes?
Berapa menit?

> For five minutes.
> **Selama lima menit.**
>
> Fifteen minutes ago.
> **Lima belas menit yang lalu.**

My watch has stopped.
Jam saya mati.

My watch is broken.
Jam saya rusak.

My watch is slow.
Jam saya lambat.

My watch is fast.
Jam saya cepat.

The clock is correct.
Jamnya benar.

The clock is wrong.
Jamnya salah.

early	**kepagian**
late	**terlambat**
on time	**tepat**

There is a common Indonesian saying for being late: *Jam karet.* It means "rubber watch."

Days of the Week

Sunday	**Minggu**
Monday	**Senin**
Tuesday	**Selasa**
Wednesday	**Rabu**
Thursday	**Kamis**
Friday	**Jumat**
Saturday	**Sabtu**

One may precede the name for the day of the week with the word *hari*, for example, *hari Senin*, *hari Selasa*, etc.

What day is it today?
Hari apa hari ini?

Today is Monday.
Hari ini hari Senin.

What day is it tomorrow?
Hari apa besok?
Besok hari apa?

Tomorrow is Tuesday.
Besok hari Selasa.

On Wednesday.
Pada hari Rabu.

On Sundays.
Setiap hari Minggu.

Every Friday.
Setiap hari Jum'at.

Last Tuesday.
Hari Selasa yang lalu.

Next Monday.
Hari Senin depan.

Common terms:

today	**hari ini**
two days ago	**dua hari yang lalu**
yesterday	**kemarin**
tomorrow	**besok**
day after tomorrow	**lusa, besok lusa**
a/one week	**satu minggu, seminggu**
last week	**minggu yang lalu**
a week ago	**seminggu yang lalu**
three weeks ago	**tiga minggu yang lalu**
next week	**minggu depan**
every week	**setiap minggu, tiap-tiap minggu**
weekly	**mingguan**
once a week	**seminggu sekali**
twice a week	**dua kali seminggu**
dawn	**subuh, fajar**
morning	**pagi**

early morning	**pagi-pagi**
in the morning	**pada pagi hari, besok pagi**
this morning	**pagi ini, tadi pagi**
yesterday morning	**kemarin pagi**
tomorrow morning	**besok pagi**
noon, midday	**siang hari**
at noon	**pada siang hari**
afternoon	**sore**
this afternoon	**sore ini, nanti sore**
in the afternoon	**pada sore hari**
yesterday afternoon	**kemarin sore**
tomorrow afternoon	**besok sore**
eve, evening	**malam**
this evening	**malam ini, nanti malam**
yesterday evening	**kemarin malam,**
	tadi malam
tomorrow evening	**besok malam**
Christmas Eve	**Malam Natal**
New Year's Eve	**Malam Tahun Baru**
night	**malam**
at night	**pada malam hari**
tonight	**malam ini**
last night	**tadi malam**
two nights ago	**dua malam yang lalu**
midnight	**tengah malam**
year	**tahun**
leap year	**tahun kabisat**
last year, a year ago	**setahun/satu tahun**
	yang lalu
two years ago	**dua tahun yang lalu**
next year	**tahun depan**
this year	**tahun ini**
every year	**setiap tahun,**
	tiap-tiap tahun
once a year	**sekali setahun**
twice a year	**dua kali setahun**

What year?
Tahun berapa?

In 1961.
Pada tahun sembilan ratus enam puluh satu.
Pada tahun sembilan belas enam satu.

In 1970.
Pada tahun sembilan belas tujuh puluh.

In 2000.
Pada tahun dua ribu.

SEASONS & WEATHER

Seasons

What season is this now?
Sekarang musim apa?

It is now (the) …
Sekarang …

winter	**musim dingin, musim salju**
in winter	**pada musim dingin**
spring	**musim semi**
summer	**musim panas**
fall	**musim gugur**
rainy season	**musim penghujan, musim hujan**
dry season	**musim kemarau, musim kering**

Weather

How is the weather today?
Bagaimana cuaca hari ini?
Bagaimana hawa hari ini?

What's the weather like?
Bagaimana cuacanya?

It's sunny.
Banyak matahari.

It's windy.
Berangin, banyak angin.

It's foggy.
Berkabut kabut.

It's foggy/misty.
Banyak kabut.

It's raining (hard).
Hujan (deras).

It's drizzling.
Hujan rintik-rintik.

It's snowing.
Turun salju.

It's cold.
Dingin.
Hawanya dingin.

It's hot.
Panas.
Hawanya panas.

It's too hot.
Terlalu panas.

It's not too hot.
Tidak terlalu panas.

It's humid.
Lembab.
Hawanya lembab.

It's nice.
Cuacanya.
Hawanya bagus.

It's going to rain.
Mau hujan.

It's always hot.
Selalu panas.

Sometimes it is cold.
Kadang-kadang dingin.

Common terms:

dew	**embun**
fog	**kabut**
hurricane	**angin topan**
mist	**kabut**
rain	**hujan**
snow	**salju**
tornado	**angin topan**
typhoon	**angin puyuh**
wind	**angin**
breeze	**angin sepoi-sepoi**
cold wind	**angin dingin**
hard wind	**angin kencang,**
	angin keras

Other Indonesian Titles
from Hippocrene

Speak Standard Indonesian:
A Beginner's Guide
Liaw Yock Fang

"… a useful and dependable guide to spoken Indonesian." —*New Straights Times*

Designed for both the student and the traveler, this guide presents over 200 dialogue exercises that will help to overcome daily communication obstacles in Indonesia, including meeting new acquaintances, identifying and describing objects, making appointments, dealing with the practical nitty-gritties of traveling and settling down in an Indonesian-speaking society.

285 pages · 5 x 7½ · $11.95 pb · 0-7818-0186-9 · (159)

Indonesian-English/English-Indonesian
Practical Dictionary

289 pages · 4½ x 7 · $11.95 pb · 0-87052-810-6 · (127)

Other Hippocrene Titles of
Regional Interest

Flavors of Burma: Cuisine and Culture
from the Land of Golden Pagodas
Susan Chan

Burma's typical meals include rice, curries, salads, vegetables, and side dishes such as cucumber and tomato slices eaten with traditional Burmese fish sauce (*Nga-Pi-Yae*) and Fried Shrimp with Shrimp Paste (*Balachung*), which are presented here in 76 enticing recipes. The author depicts the culture and traditions of Burma, providing ample information on the Burmese market, commonly used ingredients, and eating and serving customs, explaining, for example, that Burmese eat with their fingertips. She also familiarizes her readers with the language, festivals, and principal cities of this country.

221 pages · 6 x 9 · $22.50 hc · 0-7818-0947-9 · (403)

Fine Filipino Food

Karen Hulene Bartell

Created from recipes collected during the author's travels to this country at the crossroads of the Pacific Ocean and the South China and Sulu seas, *Fine Filipino Food* is a testament to a rich mix of cultures. Chinese traders introduced stir-frying and deep-frying cooking techniques, as well as noodles and soy products; Malaysian spice traders brought seasonings from the Spice Islands and introduced that delectable appetizer, satay; adobo, arguably the best-known Filipino dish, is a by-product of both Spanish and Chinese influence. Finally, the American influence left the legacies of speed and convenience.

256 pages · 6½ x 9½ · $24.95 hc · 0-7818-0964-9 · (531)

The Best of Regional Thai Cuisine

Chef Chat Mingkwan takes the reader-chef on a culinary tour of his home country, offering favorites from each of Thailand's four regions: the cool, mountainous North, where "Curried Egg noodles" are the signature dish; the drier Northeast (Isan) where resourceful chefs rely on staples like glutinous rice and dried fish; the fertile Central region, which is home to Bangkok, abundant with seafood as well as fruits and vegetables; and the tropical South where locally grown coconut is a popular ingredient and where the majority of Thailand's Muslim population is concentrated, thus making seafood and chicken curries the classic dishes of the region.

216 pages · 6 x 9½ · $24.95 hc · 0-7818-0963-0 · (26)

Simple Laotian Cooking

Simple Laotian Cooking offers 172 recipes, including a section on the traditional Lob, a dish usually made with beef but also with chicken, fish, or wild game, which is reserved for holidays and special occasions. Served with sticky rice and fresh vegetables, it is one of the few dishes accompanied by wine. A glossary defines staple ingredients like bamboo shoots, cilantro, coconut milk, fresh ginger, kaffir lime leaves, and lemongrass. The author also incorporates western ingredients in her dishes, making Laotian cuisine even easier to cook.

225 pages · 6½ x 9½ · $24.95 hc · 0-7818-0880-4 · (522)

A Vietnamese Kitchen: Treasured Family Recipes

Ha Roda

The authentic family recipes included in *A Vietnamese Kitchen* capture the country's home cooking at its best. Steaming bowls of pho, the ever-popular beef noodle soup, spring rolls, clay pot ginger chicken, and exotic desserts such as crumpled sweet rice and banana coconut pudding are just a few of the delicacies included. The recipes are designed for the American home kitchen, and are accompanied by an introduction to Vietnamese culture and a glossary of Vietnamese culinary terms.

181 pages · 6 x 9 · $24.95 hc · 0-7818-1081-7 · (115)

Cambodian-English/English-Cambodian Standard Dictionary

355 pages · 5½ x 8¼ · $18.95 pb · 0-8705-2818-1 · (143)

Chinese-English/English-Chinese Dictionary & Phrasebook (Mandarin)

300 pages · 4 x 7½ · $12.95 pb · 0-7818-1135-X · (297)

English-Chinese Pinyin Dictionary

837 pages · 4 x 6 · $19.95 pb · 0-7818-0427-2 · (509)

Beginner's Chinese with 2 Audio CDs

175 pages · 5 x 8 · $25.95 pb · 0-7818-1095-7 · (174)

Ilocano-English/English-Ilocano Dictionary & Phrasebook

263 pages · 5 x 8 · $16.95 pb · 0-7818-0642-9 · (718)

Children's Illustrated Japanese Dictionary

94 pages · 5½ x 11 · $11.95 pb · 0-7818-0849-9 · (664)

Japanese-English/English-Japanese Concise Dictionary, Romanized

235 pages · 4 x 6 · $11.95 pb · 0-7818-0162-1 · (474)

Beginner's Japanese with 2 Audio CDs

290 pages · 5½ x 8 · $29.95 pb · 0-7818-1141-4 · (249)

Korean-English/English-Korean Practical Dictionary

355 pages · 4¼ x 8 · $19.95 pb · 0-8705-2092-X · (399)

Korean-English/English-Korean Dictionary & Phrasebook

312 pages · 3½ x 7½ · $12.95 pb · 0-7818-1029-9 · (565)

Lao-English/English-Lao Dictionary and Phrasebook
206 pages · 4 x 7 · $12.95 pb · 0-7818-0858-8 · (179)

Pilipino-English/English-Pilipino Concise Dictionary
389 pages · 4 x 6 · $12.95 pb · 0-8705-2491-7 · (393)

Pilipino-English/English-Pilipino Dictionary and Phrasebook
186 pages · 3½ x 7 · $11.95 pb · 0-7818-0451-5 · (295)

Concise Sanskrit-English Dictionary
366 pages · 4 x 6 · $14.95 pb · 0-7818-0203-2 · (605)

Tagalog-English/English-Tagalog (Pilipino) Standard Dictionary
461 pages · 4 x 6 · $21.95 pb · 0-7818-0960-6 · (388)

Beginner's Vietnamese
515 pages · 5¼ x 8 · $19.95 pb · 0-7818-0411-6 · (253)

Vietnamese-English/ English-Vietnamese Standard Dictionary
889 pages · 5¼ x 8 · $24.95 pb · 0-8705-2924-2 · (529)

Vietnamese-English/ English-Vietnamese Dictionary and Phrasebook
245 pages · 3½ x 7½ · $11.95 pb · 0-7818-0991-6 · (104)